"*Finish the Mission* issues a clarion reminder of God's enduring passion to glorify himself by blessing all nations on earth. The gospel and mission are inseparable. A clear understanding of the mission of the church is absolutely essential in today's fast-changing global environment."

Steve Richardson, President, Pioneers-USA

"What will it take to finish the mission? Gospel seed must fall into the ground and die. Lord Jesus, through these heart-exposing pages, would you thrust out thousands of risk-taking disciples to the ends of the earth? May this compelling admonition jolt the church out of com placency and into the gathering of your sheep from among the earth's peoples."

David Sitton, President, To Every Tribe; author, *Reckless Abandon* and *To Every Tribe with Jesus*

"God defines marriage and God defines mission. *Finish the Mission* is a vital proclamation of an emphasis that even evangelicals dodge— mostly out of embarrassment. Putting God's opinions above all others, the authors portray well God's rescue operation to the peoples who still have no friend to help them comprehend the Easter story. As John Piper says, '*We're concerned for all suffering, but especially* eternal *suffering.*' Serious disciples will take these declarations seriously."

Greg Livingstone, Founder, Frontiers; Coordinator, Ministries to Muslims, Evangelical Presbyterian Church

FINISH THE MISSION

OTHER DESIRING GOD CONFERENCE BOOKS BY CROSSWAY:

Thinking. Loving. Doing.: A Call to Glorify God with Heart and Mind, 2011

With Calvin in the Theater of God: The Glory of Christ and Everyday Life, 2010

The Power of Words and the Wonder of God, 2009

Stand: A Call for the Endurance of the Saints, 2008

The Supremacy of Christ in a Postmodern World, 2007

Suffering and the Sovereignty of God, 2006

Sex and the Supremacy of Christ, 2005

A God-Entranced Vision of All Things: The Legacy of Jonathan Edwards, 2004

FINISH THE
MISSION

BRINGING THE GOSPEL TO THE UNREACHED AND UNENGAGED

JOHN PIPER AND
DAVID MATHIS, EDITORS

:: CROSSWAY

WHEATON, ILLINOIS

Finish the Mission: Bringing the Gospel to the Unreached and Unengaged

Copyright © 2012 by Desiring God

Published by Crossway
        1300 Crescent Street
        Wheaton, Illinois 60187

Cover design: Matthew Taylor, Taylor Design Works

First printing 2012

Printed in the United States of America

Unless otherwise indicated, Scripture quotations are from the ESV® Bible (*The Holy Bible, English Standard Version®*), copyright © 2001 by Crossway. Used by permission. All rights reserved.

Scripture quotations marked HCSB have been taken from *The Holman Christian Standard Bible®* Copyright © 1999, 2000, 2003 by Holman Bible Publishers. Used by permission.

All emphases in Scripture quotations have been added by the authors.

Trade paperback ISBN: 978-1-4335-3483-6
PDF ISBN: 978-1-4335-3484-3
Mobipocket ISBN: 978-1-4335-3485-0
ePub ISBN: 978-1-4335-3486-7

Library of Congress Cataloging-in-Publication Data

Finish the mission : bringing the Gospel to the unreached and
    unengaged / John Piper and David Mathis, editors.
        p.   cm.
    Includes bibliographical references and indexes.
    ISBN 978-1-4335-3483-6 (tp)
    1. Missions. 2. Evangelistic work. I. Piper, John, 1946-
II. Mathis, David, 1980-
BV2061.3.F56   2012
269'.2—dc23   2012008009

Crossway is a publishing ministry of Good News Publishers.

VP		22	21	20	19	18	17	16	15	14	13
16	15	14	13	12	11	10	9	8	7	6	5	4	3

For those who have left
house or brothers or sisters or mother
or father or children or lands,
for Jesus's sake and for the gospel
to finish the mission

CONTENTS

CONTRIBUTORS

Louie Giglio is pastor of Passion City Church in Atlanta, Georgia. As founder and leader of Passion Conferences, he travels worldwide challenging this generation, college students in particular, to a passionate pursuit of God. A graduate of Georgia State University and the Southwestern Baptist Theological Seminary, he has been at the forefront of collegiate ministry for over twenty years. Louie is author of *The Air I Breathe: Worship as a Way of Life* and *I Am Not But I Know I Am*. His wife is Shelley.

David Mathis is executive editor at Desiring God and elder at Bethlehem Baptist Church, Twin Cities, Minnesota. He is a graduate of Furman University and is completing a distance program with Reformed Theological Seminary, Orlando, Florida. He has authored articles and chapters and is coeditor of *With Calvin in the Theater of God: The Glory of Christ and Everyday Life*; *The Pastor as Scholar and the Scholar as Pastor: Reflections on Life and Ministry*; and *Thinking. Loving. Doing.: A Call to Glorify God with Heart and Mind*. He and his wife, Megan, have twin sons, Carson and Coleman.

Michael Oh is president and founder of CBI Japan, which includes a graduate-level theological seminary (Christ Bible Seminary), church planting efforts (All Nations Fellowship), and various outreach ministries, including a youth outreach called the Heart & Soul Cafe. Michael is a graduate of the University of Pennsylvania and Trinity Evangelical Divinity School; he also completed a master's degree in Japanese Studies at Harvard University. Since 2007 he has served on the Board of the Lausanne Movement for world evangelization. He and his wife, Pearl, have five children.

John Piper is pastor for preaching and vision at Bethlehem Baptist Church, where he has served since 1980. A graduate of Wheaton College, Fuller Seminary, and the University of Munich, he is author of over forty books, including *Desiring God*; *The Pleasures of God*; *Don't Waste Your Life*; *Seeing and Savoring Jesus Christ*; *God Is the Gospel*; *Think*; *Bloodlines*; and the widely acclaimed missions title *Let the Nations Be Glad!*. John and his wife, Noël, have five children and twelve grandchildren.

David Platt is pastor of The Church at Brook Hills, Birmingham, Alabama. Previously he served as dean of chapel and assistant professor of expository preaching and apologetics at New Orleans Baptist Theological Seminary, as well as staff evangelist at Edgewater Baptist Church in New Orleans. A graduate of the University of Georgia and New Orleans Baptist Theological Seminary, he is author of *Radical: Taking Back Your Faith from the American Dream* and *Radical Together: Unleashing* *the People of God for the Purpose of God.* David and his wife, Heather, have two sons, Joshua and Caleb.

Michael Ramsden has been the European director of RZIM Zacharias Trust since it was founded in 1997. A passionate evangelist and apologist, he is also lecturer in Christian apologetics at Wycliffe Hall, Oxford University, where his main involvement is with the Oxford Centre for Christian Apologetics. He travels widely, speaking at universities, churches, and conferences. He and his wife, Anne, have three children.

Ed Stetzer serves as the vice president of research and ministry development for Lifeway Christian Resources. He has planted churches in New York, Pennsylvania, and Georgia and trained church planters on five continents. He is the author of many articles and books including *Planting New Churches in a Postmodern Age, Strategic Outreach* (with Eric Ramsey), *Breaking the Missional Code* (with David Putman), and *Planting Missional Churches.* He is also a visiting professor at Trinity Evangelical Divinity School and the Southeastern Baptist Theological Seminary. He and his wife, Donna, have three daughters.

INTRODUCTION

Remember, Jesus Never Lies

David Mathis

Remember, Jesus never lies. *Never.*

That God "never lies" (Titus 1:2) was an important reminder for Paul's protégé, ministering among the Cretans, who were, by the admission of one of their own, "always liars, evil beasts, lazy gluttons" (v. 12). Paul says to Titus: *Remember, God never lies.*

And it's an important reminder for us, nearly two millennia later, especially in regard to the mission the God-man started with his own life, inaugurated in his own death, sealed with his own resurrection, launched in his Great Commission, and promised to bring to completion. The Holy Spirit says to the churches: *Remember, Jesus never lies.*

Jesus himself has promised—just as surely as he declares over his work of redemption, "It is finished" (John 19:30)—that also his one-day-soon triumphant bride will declare with him over the application of that work in global missions, "It is finished." The Commission will be completed.

THE MISSION WILL FINISH

In prelude to his Great Commission, Jesus says that *all authority* in heaven and on earth has been given to him (Matt. 28:18). Having taken our flesh and blood, and fulfilled the destiny of humanity (Ps. 8:3–8; Heb. 2:5–10) along his sacrificial course, the man Christ Jesus now rules the whole universe (our little globe included) with the very sovereignty of God, ensuring the success of his global mission.

Against all suspicions to the contrary, the sovereign Christ will not be thwarted in carrying out his promise, "I will build my church, and the gates of hell shall not prevail against it" (Matt. 16:18). The God-man, risen and reigning, most assuredly will make good on the pledge that his gospel "will be proclaimed throughout the whole world as a testimony to all nations, and then the end will come" (Matt. 24:14). Wielding the indomitable strength of his divinity, he is poised to guarantee—with absolute certainty—the fulfillment of Habakkuk 2:14: "The earth will be filled with the knowledge of the glory of the LORD as the waters cover the sea."[1]

MISSIONS: ALL ABOUT THIS JESUS

At the end of the day, global missions is about the worship of this spectacular Jesus. The goal of missions is the worldwide worship of the God-man by his redeemed people from every tribe, tongue, and nation. The outcome of missions is all peoples delighting to praise Jesus. And the motivation for missions is the enjoyment that his people have in him. Missions aims at, brings about, and is fueled by the worship of Jesus.

Another way to say it is that missions is about Jesus's global glory. From beginning to end—in target, effect, and impetus— missions centers on the worldwide fame of the Messiah in the praises of his diverse peoples from every tribe, tongue, and nation. What's at stake in missions is the universal honor of the Father in the global glory of his Son in the joy of all the peoples.

WHAT IS MISSIONS?[2]

Rooted in the Latin *mitto* (meaning "to send"), *missions* is the half-millennium-old English term signifying the *sending* of Jesus's followers into his global harvest of all peoples. For nearly

---

[1] Which, I presume, prompted Jared Wilson to tweet on February 4, 2012, "If you hold the gospel up to your ear, you can hear the roaring waves of Habakkuk 2:14." I'd never seen a tweet quoted in a printed book until reading Wilson's excellent *Gospel Wakefulness*, so it seemed it might be fitting to mention his tweet here.

[2] A version of this introduction first appeared as chapter 18, "Missions," in *Don't Call It a Comeback: An Old Faith for a New Day*, ed. Kevin DeYoung (Wheaton, IL: Crossway, 2011).

three hundred years, the term *missions* has been used in particular for world evangelization, for pioneering the gospel among the peoples to whom it has yet to advance.

Among others, two passages in the Gospel of Matthew get to the heart of missions. Jesus says to his disciples in Matthew 9:37–38, "The harvest is plentiful, but the laborers are few; therefore pray earnestly to the Lord of the harvest to *send out* laborers into his harvest." Missions means *sending out* workers into the global harvest.

A second passage is Jesus's sending out of his disciples in Matthew 28:18–20, the epic-making summons we call "the Great Commission." Here Jesus's main command, "make disciples of all nations," follows the charge to "go"—to be *sent out*. Sending out and going are two sides of the same coin. Jesus and his established church send out, and those who go are "the sent ones," or "missionaries." So *missions* is the church's sending out of missionaries (the sent ones) to pioneer the church among peoples who otherwise have no access to the gospel.

THE COMMISSION

Perhaps as good a way forward as any in this introduction is to walk just briefly through this Great Commission that gets at the heart of the missionary enterprise.

> And Jesus came and said to [his disciples], "All authority in heaven and on earth has been given to me. Go therefore and make disciples of all nations, baptizing them in the name of the Father and of the Son and of the Holy Spirit, teaching them to observe all that I have commanded you. And behold, I am with you always, to the end of the age." (Matt. 28:18–20)

"DISCIPLE ALL NATIONS" (V. 19)

We've noted already Jesus's claim to "all authority" (v. 18). In view of such unmatched authority, he then draws out an implication for his followers in verse 19—one of the most important *therefores* in the history of the world. "Go *therefore* and make disciples of all nations . . ."

The two commands in our English—"go" and "make disciples of all nations"—work together as one charge in the original language. A literal translation would be something like, "having gone, disciple all nations." The main emphasis falls on discipling, but the going is necessary. In order to engage in this worldwide task of discipling all nations, there must be going. Jesus emphatically does not promise that all nations will come to Jerusalem so that his disciples can merely invest themselves where they are. They will need to go. There are oceans and borders to cross, languages to learn, cultural divides to bridge. Like Paul and Barnabas in Antioch, they should be "sent off" (Acts 13:3) gladly by the church for such work. There must be missionaries.

But even in our current global context, where unreached peoples are clustering in cities where churches already are established, another kind of going must happen: being "sent out" from ordinary, everyday life among people just like us to invest in the difficult spade work of language learning and culture crossing. Even where geography isn't an issue, culture and language are. So the Commission necessitates goings of all sorts.

Disciple Is a Verb

If Jesus's charge to "make disciples of all nations" is the heart of the Commission, what does he mean by this discipling? It is clear that he does not mean the mere pursuit of conversion. That won't work with what follows: ". . . baptizing them in the name of the Father and of the Son of the Holy Spirit, teaching them to observe all that I have commanded you." Teaching the nations "to observe all that I have commanded you" is not the mere pursuit of conversion. And if discipling all nations doesn't mean simple classroom information transfer, as we're prone to think in the West, but "teaching to observe," what must it involve?

At least it must aim at a kind of lived-out spiritual maturity. This is how many well-meaning Christians today use the term *discipleship*—as a term for pursuing spiritual maturity. Being a "disciple," they say, means being a serious, rather than a casual, follower of Jesus. "Discipleship programs" are designed for those intentionally seeking Christian growth, so it goes. Maybe. But something seems to be lacking here, at least as an explanation of what the Commission is getting at.

Jesus's Example

Within the context of Matthew's Gospel, is there not more to say? Does "disciple all nations" not call to mind how Jesus himself discipled his men? They were, after all, his disciples. And when they heard him say, "disciple all nations," would they not think this discipling is similar to the very thing he did with them—investing prolonged, real-life, day-in, day-out, intentional time with younger believers in order to personally grow them to maturity, as well as model for them how to *disciple* others in the same way?

This sounds like what Paul is getting at in 2 Timothy 2:2, when he instructs his disciple Timothy, "What you have heard from me in the presence of many witnesses entrust to faithful men who will be able to teach others also." *Timothy, my disciple, disciple others to disciple others.* Four spiritual generations get explicit mention here: Paul, Timothy, "faithful men," and "others also"—with the implication that further generations are to follow.[3]

Discipling, seen in this light, means not merely the pursuit of our own spiritual maturity but getting outside ourselves for personal connection and substantial, intentional investment of time in a few others—the kind of investment for which there must be *going* to accomplish among the nations. Jesus spent over three years with his twelve disciples. He called them to be discipled at the outset of his ministry (Matt. 4:19), and he gave them the lion's share of his life until his departure in Matthew 28. He invested his life in his men. It is eye-opening to track in the Gospels how

---

[3] For more on disciple making and its important place in finishing the mission, see the appendix, "What Next? Disciple a Few."

much Jesus gave of himself to his disciples. While the crowds pursued him, he pursued his disciples. He was willing to bless the masses, but he invested in the few.

All Nations

But if "disciple" refers not merely to conversion and personal spiritual maturity but to the personal investment of the discipler's life in others, what about "all nations"? Here Jesus has struck a note that is part of a biblical symphony spanning the Scriptures from Genesis to Revelation.

From creation, God has been concerned with "all the nations." The genealogies of Genesis trace the origin of all nations from Adam through Noah and his sons (Genesis 10). And with his blessing of all nations in mind, God called a moon worshiper named Abram to "Go from your country . . . to the land that I will show you. And I will make of you a great nation . . . and in you all the families of the earth shall be blessed" (Gen. 12:1–3). Note the word "all."

From Abram (renamed Abraham, "the father of a multitude of nations," in Gen. 17:4–5) would come God's chosen nation called "Israel." This nation's special relationship with God was to bring about blessing to those of the rest of the world's nations who were separated from their creator going back to their father Adam.

For the sake of the nations, God worked on this one nation for two thousand years. He multiplied her number, delivered her from slavery, led her through the wilderness, defeated her enemies, established her in a promised land, and brought her to her highest point of peace and prosperity under the kingship of David and his son Solomon. With foes defeated and the temple complete, it looked as if God's blessing was now poised to flow to the nations through Israel's flourishing and the nations' submission to her.

Come and See

In 1 Kings 4, Israel has become "as many as the sand by the sea" (v. 20). Solomon is ruling "over all the kingdoms from the

Euphrates to the land of the Philistines and to the border of Egypt" (v. 21) and said to have "dominion over all the region west of the Euphrates" (v. 24). Is this the fulfillment of God's promises to Abram in Genesis 12:3 and 15:5 to make his descendants as numerous as the stars and to bless the nations through his off- spring? Has God brought all his purposes to pass in Israel's prosperity so that now climactically "all the peoples of the earth may know that the LORD is God" (1 Kings 8:60)?

But the sin problem that began with Adam still remained, with Israel herself suffering from the same sinful condition as all the nations. Just as the nations needed the blessing of forgiveness, a new heart, final removal of divine wrath, and restoration to God himself, so also did Israel. And 1 Kings 11 to 2 Kings 25 catalogs how sin destroyed Israel over the course of several hundred years, as she fell from the height of Solomon's reign to the utter depths in the destruction of Jerusalem and in exile under the Babylonians.

But the prophets, even amidst their strong denunciations, promised stunning hope beyond the exile for the remnant that would return to God. And it wouldn't be the mere restoration to Israel's former days, for as the prophet Isaiah announced, "It is too light a thing that you should be my servant to raise up the tribes of Jacob and to bring back the preserved of Israel; I will make you as a light for the nations, that my salvation may reach to the end of the earth" (Isa. 49:6).

God had more in mind for the blessing of the nations than "Come and see Israel and eat from her scraps." In the Great Commission, we find Jesus's monumental revelation to his followers—and through them to the world—of the mission for world blessing that God has had in store from the beginning: God's people knowing and enjoying him in Jesus and going and telling all the nations about him.

As Jesus prepares to go to the cross, he is the one who promises, "This gospel of the kingdom will be proclaimed throughout the whole world as a testimony to all nations" (Matt. 24:14). And

Jesus is the one who charges his disciples to "make disciples of all nations" and promised them, "You will receive power when the Holy Spirit has come upon you, and you will be my witnesses in Jerusalem and in all Judea and Samaria, and to the end of the earth" (Acts 1:8).

Go and Disciple

Jesus himself has ushered in a new season of world history in which God is no longer focusing his preparatory redemptive action on Israel in a come-and-see fashion (when "in past generations he allowed all the nations to walk in their own ways," Acts 14:16). But now with the full accomplishment of the gospel of his Son, God has widened his redemptive lens, so to speak, to all the nations and inaugurated the Spirit-empowered age of go and tell—or better yet, go and disciple.

The apostle Paul says that the essence of his ministry is "to bring about the obedience of faith for the sake of [Jesus's] name among *all the nations*" (Rom. 1:5) and that the gospel is now being "made known to *all nations*" (Rom. 16:26). God's global purpose, being exercised through the authority of the risen and reigning God-man, is to make worshipers of his Son among *all the nations*—every tribe and tongue and people.

When Jesus grants John a glimpse of the end, he hears a new song: "Worthy are you to take the scroll and to open its seals, for you were slain, and by your blood you ransomed people for God *from every tribe and language and people and nation*" (Rev. 5:9). Two chapters later, he sees "a great multitude that no one could number, *from every nation, from all tribes and peoples and languages*, standing [in worship] before the throne and before the Lamb" (Rev. 7:9–10).

The Post-Christian West and the Global South

In the course of pursuing all nations, Paul brought the gospel to Philippi (Acts 16) and beyond, and for the next seventeen-plus centuries, Christianity took root particularly in the West

(Europe and eventually North America). The sixteenth-century Reformation deepened the roots in many respects, but the horrific seventeenth-century religious wars fed the eighteenth-century "Enlightenment" and with it, in time, modernism and secularism.

Today the West, once the stronghold of global Christianity, is becoming increasingly (and quickly) post-Christian. There are pockets of significant blessing and great hope for advance in the days ahead, but by and large the church that once stood at the center of Western society is finding herself at the periphery (which, in God's economy, may be a very good thing for the Western church).

But the decline of Christianity in the West has not meant global decline for the gospel. Jesus will build his church. And *remember, Jesus never lies.* The last fifty years have produced a stunning and historic global development as Christianity has blossomed in Africa, Latin America, and Asia—in what many are calling "the Global South." The figures can be misleading since they can report only *professing* Christians, but even allowing for significant inflation, the general trend is astonishing:

- Europe was home to over 70 percent of the world's professing Christians in 1900, but by 2000, it was less than 30 percent. In the meantime, Latin America and Africa had become home to over 40 percent.
- Africa had ten million professing Christians in 1900—about 10 percent of the population. But by 2000, the number was 360 million—about half the African population. This may mark the largest shift in religious affiliation in world history.[4]
- "The number of practicing Christians in China is approaching the number in the United States."[5]
- "Last Sunday . . . more Christian believers attended church in China than in all of so-called 'Christian Europe.'"[6]
- "In a word, the Christian church has experienced a larger geographical redistribution in the last fifty years than in any comparable period in its history, with the exception of the very earliest years of church history."[7]

---

[4] Philip Jenkins, "Believing in the Global South," *First Things* (December 2006): 13.
[5] Mark Noll, *The New Shape of World Christianity: How American Experience Reflects Global Faith* (Downers Grove, IL: IVP Academic, 2009), 10.
[6] Ibid.
[7] Ibid.

Going with the Global South

This amazing trend raises the question for some as to whether the West is done sending missionaries. Will it not now be left to the Global South to finish the mission? The clear answer is no. First, don't discount the power of gospel-advancing partnerships between the West and the Global South. But, second, these partnerships should not mean merely sending Western money, but Western people. Going is necessary for discipling.

According to the Joshua Project, which tracks the global progress of the gospel among the world's unreached peoples, there are an estimated seven thousand unreached people groups in the world out of a total of about seventeen thousand ethno-linguistic peoples.[8] The Joshua Project lists over 1,500 of these unreached peoples as *unengaged*, meaning that there is no current missionary work among them. With so much work yet to be done, it will take the gospel partnership of the whole global church—Western, Hispanic, Asian, African, Eastern European, Russian, Brazilian, Middle Eastern, and more—to take the message about Jesus to the world's final missionary frontier, the peoples most hostile to the gospel. As Michael Oh shows us in chapter 4, missions today is no longer from West to East, and North to South, but "from every land to every land."

Not only does this new global situation create promise for new ways of partnering both in sending people and resources, but also it gives rise to new possibilities and problems in the West.

The Promise and Potential Danger of "Missional"

In the last decade, a new term related to *missions* has come into use among evangelicals doing domestic ministry: *missional*. The most insightful of those using the term recognize that the West is quickly becoming post-Christian and that this shift raises important questions about what it means to do domestic ministry. Europe and North America have become more and more like a

---

[8] http://www.JoshuaProject.net.

mission field—but a post-Christian, rather than a pre-Christian, field. Since the term *evangelism* carries for some the baggage (and narrowness) of Christendom days when the general biblical worldview was prevalent enough in society that street-corner confrontations and stadium crusades found more traction and produced more genuine converts, the emergence of the term *missional* (somewhat in place of *evangelistic*) signifies that the times are changing in some significant degree, calling for new missions-like engagement and evangelistic holism. This fresh thinking is a good development, but with it comes a danger.

The danger is that with the discussions about "being missional" and "every Christian being a missionary," the pursuit of all the peoples by prioritizing the unreached can be obscured. The contributors to this book are eager for us *both* to live "on mission" among our native people *and* to preserve a place for the biblical category of reaching the unreached. The biblical theme is not merely that God reaches as many *people* as possible, but *all the peoples.* He intends to create worshipers of his Son from every tribe, tongue, and nation. The push for being *missional* captures something very important in the heart of God, but this is dangerous when it comes at the cost of something else essential in the heart of God: pursuing *all the nations*, not merely those who share our language and culture.

Prioritizing the Unreached

As Ed Stetzer will argue in chapter 5, we need a solid *both-and.* Our churches should pursue both *mission* among our own people and *missions* among the world's unreached peoples. One way to sum it up is to say that we can't be truly *missional* without preserving a prominent place for the pursuit of the unreached. It doesn't matter how much a church may say that she is being *missional*; she is not fully *missional* in the biblical sense if she is not pursuing mission at home (traditionally called *evangelism*) among her native reached people as well as being an engaged sender in support of missionaries to the unreached.

As the West grows increasingly post-Christian, it is easy to see the obvious need for the gospel opening up around us to the neglect of the frontiers. Missions is a summons to the frontiers. And more and more those frontiers aren't savages living in the woods that make for the missions stories of the previous generation, like *Bruchko, Peace Child,* and *Through Gates of Splendor.* Today's "frontiers" are home to those most hostile to the gospel. Don't think jungles and loin clothes. Think flat, hot, and crowded in the world's urban mega-centers. It seems God is bringing the unreached peoples out of the woods and into the cities for the finishing of the mission.

There Will Be Suffering and Martyrdom

All this means there will be suffering. Many of the estimated seven thousand unreached peoples (and the more than 1,500 unengaged peoples) are unreached (and unengaged) for a reason. They are profoundly hostile to the gospel. But the suffering and the martyrdom to come—and they will come[9]—will not be a setback for our sovereign Savior.

Not only is suffering the consequence of finishing the mission, but it is God's appointed means by which he will show the superior worth of his Son to all the peoples. Just as it was "fitting that he . . . should make the founder of [our] salvation perfect through suffering" (Heb. 2:10), so it is fitting that God save a people from all the peoples from eternal suffering through the redemptive suffering of Jesus displayed in the temporal sufferings of his missionaries.

This is why Paul could rejoice in his sufferings—because he knew that in them he was "filling up what is lacking in Christ's afflictions" (Col. 1:24). What is lacking in Jesus's sufferings is not redemptive value but personal presentation to the peoples he died to save. And in the sufferings and martyrdoms of missions,

---

[9] It is generally accepted that there were more Christian martyrs in the twentieth century than in the nineteen previous centuries combined.

"the sent ones" fill up what is lacking by showing Jesus's superior value and pointing to his sufferings in their own.

So the call to finish the mission is unavoidably a call for martyrs—not a call for kamikazes but a call for missionaries bent on Jesus's worldwide fame and satisfied so deeply in him that they can say with Esther, "If I perish, I perish" (Est. 4:16) and with Paul, "To die is gain" (Phil. 1:21).

JESUS WILL BE WITH US (V. 20)

The power for life-reorienting giving for missions and life-risking going in missions, for suffering and for martyrdom, is the enjoyment of the One whom we preach. Not only is missions powered by Jesus's universal authority, founded on his finished work, and modeled in his ministry, but also missions is sustained by the promise of his presence and the pleasure we have in him. He says "behold" to make sure he has our attention, because this is really precious. "*Behold*, I am with you always, to the end of the age."

He will be with you. At the border of the "closed" country, in the learning of an arduous language, and in the disorientation of a new culture, he will be with you. In speaking the gospel when your hearers may turn on you, in persecution, and in jail, he will be with you. And when you're pressed to renounce the faith or die, he will be with you. He loves to be with his people to give them the grace to say with Martin Luther, from the heart,

Let goods and kindred go,
This mortal life also.
The body they may kill;
God's truth abideth still.
His kingdom is forever.

Missions is about the worship of Jesus and the joy of all peoples. And as surely as Jesus is Lord of the universe, the mission will finish. He will build his church. He will be worshiped among every people. And in him will his redeemed people, from all the peoples, forever "rejoice with joy that is inexpressible and filled with glory" (1 Pet. 1:8).

LET'S FINISH THE MISSION

With this awe-inspiring aim in view, our contributors take up the mantle of the Great Commission and its Spirit-powered completion. The theme isn't new, but you might find the approach refreshing.

Chapter 1 is a surprising start to a book on missions. We'll join Louie Giglio as he takes a step back from the global-missions summons to adjust our perspective about the bigness and supremacy of our galactic God. He notes that Isaiah amazingly overheard the God of unparalleled majesty ask, "Whom shall I send, and who will go for us?" (Isa. 6:8), and Giglio awakens us to how the heavens are telling the glory of the mind-bogglingly impressive and powerful God behind the missionary invitation—the one who gives the mission and promises to finish it is utterly unmatched in his grandeur and strength.

David Platt (chapter 2) then sobers us with the biblical and terrifying reality of hell and the tragic lostness of billions worldwide who do not know the living God through the gospel of his unique Son. Platt serves us with the thoroughness of a careful theologian, providing biblical text after text, mixed with the gentleness and concern of an experienced pastor.

You don't typically expect much by way of apologetics in a missions book, but then Michael Ramsden is no typical missionary. Ramsden's approach (chapter 3) to the theme of courage is substantively inspiring. He doesn't just tell us to be courageous, as such a mission requires, but he builds courage into our minds and hearts as he addresses the reasonableness and solidity of biblical revelation and the Christian worldview, all set carefully within the context of global mission by a worldwide traveler who goes regularly on gospel mission into places he can't mention publicly.

Michael Oh (chapter 4) then comes to us from Japan, living among one of the world's hardest-to-reach peoples. As he walks us through a powerful exposition of the Lord's Prayer, he seeks to awaken us to how non-Western nations (Korea, Brazil, and others) are surpassing most Western locales in sending power for Jesus's global cause. The mission force is perhaps much larger than we're prone to think.

Chapter 5 reminds us that we've been *sent*. There's no getting around it. No matter what city, state, or country you're residing in as you read this book, you haven't always been there. At some point relatively recently, whether days or decades ago, God in his exhaustive and excellent sovereignty *sent* you to the community in which you now live, work, and play. Ed Stetzer refuses to let us off the hook for laboring toward the finishing of the mission just because we live safely tucked among our native people. He argues for the importance of both global missions to the unreached and unengaged and intentional local mission wherever God has placed us.

Finally, in chapter 6, John Piper unpacks for us the great missionary song of Psalm 67. Not only does he have for us a particular word about Islam (that Christians do not worship the same God as Muslims), but also what may be an unexpected word about God's purpose in the material wealth of Christians, perhaps especially in the West. "God gives his people *material wealth* for the sake of the world's *spiritual worship*. That is, he blesses his church with riches for the sake of reaching the nations. He gives a bountiful wheat harvest for the sake of a bountiful world harvest." In other words, we are blessed to be a blessing. For Christians in the West, so many of us blessed beyond the wildest dreams of just about anyone in history, this wealth is not a curse but a blessing—unless we do not use it as God has designed, for the global advance of the gospel.

NO ORDINARY MISSIONS BOOK

So, as you can see, this is no ordinary missions book. From astronomy to exegesis, from apologetics to the Global South, from being missional at home to wielding prosperity for global cause, this group of contributors hopes to breathe a fresh fire for God's global mission into a new generation of men and women being transformed by the gospel—as well as to reignite the embers for an older generation to dream a crazy dream and finish their course investing in the eternally worthwhile pursuit of playing some small role in Jesus's unstoppable effort to complete the task.

Remember, Jesus never lies. As surely as he is God, he will finish the mission.

1

THE GALACTIC GOD WHO INVITES US INTO HIS GLORIOUS PLAN

Louie Giglio[1]

While in Kigali, Rwanda, I visited a Catholic church on the out-skirts of the city that serves as one of the many genocide memo-rials. I knew the story of Rwanda, but stepping into that place was more significant than I could have guessed. It wrecked me emotionally, and I don't think I'm going to get put back together for a while.

WRECKED IN RWANDA

Perhaps you've read the story, whether the account by the Bishop of Rwanda or any of the various historical accounts. This hap-pened in our lifetime, by the way, when we were all busy doing something else. In this particular church I visited, ten thousand men, women, and children had come for refuge thinking that the church would be a safe haven, only to be sold out by the leadership there, locked in by the militia, and systematically slaughtered over a two-day period. When you walk into this empty genocide memorial, you see victims' clothing piled on pew benches, and in a memorial grave behind the building, many of their bones are still on display. They want the bones to be seen and not forgotten.

As I walked away and processed so many things, on many levels, what I had to face at the bottom of it all is that this world

[1]Thanks to David Mathis who helped get into chapter form the transcript of my message of the same title from the 2011 Desiring God National Conference in Minneapolis, Minnesota.

is messed up at an astounding magnitude. But that's not the end of the story. At the bottom of all the mess, there is a God. There is *a* God, one God. One glorious God. An amazing, beautiful God beyond our wildest dreams and our wildest imagination. And that God has chosen to invite us close to him. In the midst of the mess, he has invited us into life with him through his gospel. Then he has chosen—crazy as it may seem—to link arms with us, in some sense, and give us all marching orders, if you will.

CHRISTIANS ARE NOT AT THEIR LEISURE

Christians are not at their leisure—that's the heartbeat of what I sense God wants me to bring in this chapter. We are not at our leisure. Rather, we are under the mandate of the grace of God— grace that found us, restored us, redeemed us, breathed life back into our dormant lungs, and brought us back from the grave for a purpose. And that purpose is that we would, with everything in us, become an amplifier of the beauty of Jesus among all the peoples on this planet. This mission is crystal clear.

There is no room for negotiating with God in taking up a book like the one you have in your hands. There should be no, *Oh, I'm just going to read this and ask the Lord to speak to my heart and see if he might want to nudge me toward his mission endeavor.* That's not an option here. There is not going to be one category for those called to the nations and then a second category for those who don't feel this is their particular thing. If we're in Jesus, all of us are in one camp, and it's the camp called "the gospel of grace." And when you receive it, you become a participator in God's global purpose. When you truly embrace the gospel, you immediately become a participator in the beautiful plan of God, whether you realize it right away or later on (maybe while reading a chapter like this).

FEET ON A ROCK, READY TO TELL

The psalmist says it like this in Psalm 40:1–2: "I waited patiently for the Lord; he inclined to me and heard my cry. He drew me up from the pit of destruction, out of the miry bog, and set my feet upon a rock, making my steps secure." He heard my cry. He heard me. And what did he do? He acted. He came down into the pit I was in. He reached out and he lifted me up. And he set my feet on a rock.

Far too many Christians put a period right there and say, *Isn't that awesome? I was in such bad shape, and Jesus reached down and brought me out. And look what he did. He put my feet on a rock, and that's awesome.* But there's more to it than that.

The gospel in Psalm 40 is the full gospel. It goes all the way out. It produces proclaimers of the story of redemption. Psalm 40:3: "He put a new song in my mouth, a song of praise to our God. Many will see and fear, and put their trust in the LORD."

"He put a new song in my mouth." So if you're not singing, you may not be saved. Psalm 40 says that he put a new song in my mouth, a hymn of praise to my God, so that *many*—not merely one person in the course of my lifetime, but many—*many* would hear and believe, putting their trust in the Lord. There is a ripple effect to the gospel that's inevitable. There's a ripple effect to true grace. It doesn't lead us to only sit and contemplate what happened to us. It leads us to proclaim what's happened to us—and what can happen to anybody and everybody on the planet.

FROM GLOBAL TO GALACTIC

The speaking assignment given to me originally was "The Global God Who Gives the Great Commission." I love that title, and I carried it in my head for a while. But toward the end of the journey, I modified it a little. I thought we could take a step back from "the global God" and think more about the galactic God. *Global* is way too small for the God we worship. God is bigger than we think he is. No matter how big you think he is, he's bigger. We barely have a clue as to the magnitude of whom we're dealing with.

And even *galactic* is too small, because galaxies are an idea that God had. I love the saying, "The universe is one of God's thoughts." True, and amazing. And I've tweaked the title to be "The Galactic God Who Invites Us into His Glorious Plan."

A FOCUS ON GOD

So let's begin this book on finishing the mission by focusing on the God who is inviting us into it. Isaiah 6 has been in my heart as I've prayed about what to say here. Isaiah 6 seems to say it all. When you have a vision, as Isaiah had, about who God is, that's all you really need. If you see what Isaiah saw, that should do it. There doesn't need to be any application at the end of a pure vision of the glory of God. When you get a vision of who God is, of his magnificence and splendor, you don't need somebody to come along and give you three steps to take. When we have a true vision, even a fleeting glimpse of the glory of God, it absolutely wrecks us but in a good way. The Spirit of God then leads us through a process of reclaiming the wreckage and putting us back together again and on a new track, the track of his glorious plan.

It seems that it all happened in a very small window of time for Isaiah. He saw the Lord. He saw him high and lifted up, not low and watered down. He saw that just the hem of the Lord's robe filled the temple. That's glory. And Isaiah saw worship happening there as these marvelous angelic beings, crying out one to the other, back and forth antiphonally, echoed the praises of God. It's not recorded here, but perhaps in the moment, Isaiah realized that worship was happening with or without him. Worship didn't begin when Isaiah showed up. It was already going on. And worship doesn't begin when you and I decide to sing a song of praise. Worship happens wherever God is present.

"WHO WILL GO FOR US?"

Here Isaiah saw something that wrecked him to the point that he said, "Woe is me!" (Isa. 6:5). He knew he was a sinner. He didn't need anybody to tell him what kind of trouble he was in. He knew that he was done. He was finished, he thought. Carry that as you read verse 6. Isaiah thinks he is on the brink of being finished when one of those beings comes flying from the altar toward him. But to his surprise, instantly transformation came—by the mercy of God.

Then he hears the voice of the Lord: "Whom shall I send, and who will go for us?" (v. 8a). Who would ever have expected that such a powerful and majestic God would ask such a question? Who knew that he would see fit to give Isaiah such a vision, wreck him in his own sinful condition, have the searing grace of God burn into his life, and then immediately have him overhear such a shocking question? *Just talking among ourselves in a triune conversation here: "Who will go for us?"* Isaiah hears the question. *What? What do you mean? You're sending somebody? Somebody's going somewhere?* "Here am I! Send me" (v. 8b).

I love the immediacy of Isaiah's response. There was no whiff of "Well, let me go home and pray about what God has for me." Let me save you the time. Let me ask you three questions: (1) Have you seen this God? I'm not asking if you've heard about him. Have you *seen* this God? (2) Have you ever felt that desperate and been touched with that kind of grace? (3) Did you hear God when he said, "Whom shall I send?" Did you hear that? Because you can't be near the cross and not hear God say it. This world is messed up on a magnitude that is staggering. People are lost, and God cares. And he's asking you, right now, "Whom shall I send? Who will go for us?"

WHO'S ASKING?

Let's back up a few steps and just think about God for a minute. Think about who's asking the question. I don't know if you've ever had someone say, "Can you move your car?" and you say, "Well, who's asking?" What an arrogant kind of me-centered world we live in. "I might move the car. Who's asking?"

So here's what I want to do in this chapter: look behind the question "Whom shall I send?" at who's asking. The question is being asked by a galactic God, who will absolutely blow your mind—a God who is being worshiped right now, I'd like for you to know, by the whole universe in the arresting fashion of the vision of Isaiah 6.

I just want you to know that the worship of God didn't start with you or with your church and its weekend gatherings. God isn't banking on our worship. He isn't saying, "I hope they sing me some songs, because I really need some worship." Seraphim are calling out, back and forth, to each other. "Holy, holy, holy is the LORD of hosts; the whole earth is full of his glory" (v. 3). God is being worshiped because he is God, and the whole created universe—in some way, shape, or form—is echoing praise to him. He is a galactic God, and the whole universe is his unrivaled symphony, and that universe is praising him like nobody's business.

HELP FROM HUBBLE

Because I want to help us grasp just a little bit of the staggering magnificence of this God whom we're dealing with (and who's asking the question "Whom shall I send?"), let me point you to a few of the amazing discoveries we're making in astronomy. The Hubble Telescope's "Ultra-Deep Field" is able to snap for us a photograph of ten thousand galaxies.

You may not be used to doing this while you're reading, but pause for a moment and check this out online. Google "Hubble" and "ten thousand galaxies" and take a good look.[2] Those are galaxies, each one of those little dots that you see on there. And if the resolution were high enough, and your eyes were good enough, you could see an innumerable number of these galaxies—each one the size of our Milky Way galaxy or bigger—all different shapes and sizes. Some of them look like a toothpick. Some of them look like a piece of jewelry. Some of them are spiral in shape, like our own galaxy.

Here's what blows my mind: Scripture says that God spoke and the universe came into being. Psalm 33:6: "By the word of the LORD the heavens were made, and by the breath of his mouth

---

[2] Or just type in the address http://www.spacetelescope.org/images/heic0406a/.

all their host." Psalm 33:9: "He spoke, and it came to be; he commanded, and it stood firm." So God, merely by the use of his voice (so to speak), made a universe, and this particular image given to us by Hubble, orbiting almost 350 miles above the earth, would be like you or me looking through an eight-foot-long straw up into the sky. That's how small a portion of the night sky is represented in this photograph. And we're looking at ten thousand galaxies—just that little portion. The God whom we worship is the creator and sovereign over such mind-boggling stretches of space and astronomical beauty.

He is the one who is asking, in case anybody wanted to know, "Whom shall I send, and who will go for us?" If you say, "Well, who wants to know?"—the Creator of all this is the one who wants to know. The galaxy-breathing God is asking.

SPECTACULAR SOMBRERO

I could point you to another image. It's from the constellation we call Virgo. This one is called the Sombrero Galaxy. Google "Hubble" and "Sombrero Galaxy" and get a look.[3] This galaxy is relatively new to us because only recently has Hubble brought the universe so close to us. The Sombrero Galaxy is staggering. It's 29,000,000 (twenty-nine million) light-years away. Pause and try to process this for a moment. A light-year is how far light travels in one year. And light is super fast. It's moving 186,000 miles a second.

By the way, we once thought that light was the fastest thing in the universe, but now we're not so sure about that. Science isn't as buttoned down as everybody wants to think it is. Don't think I am anti-science. I love science and scientists, but we shouldn't act like science is a sure bet, because nobody has yet figured out everything God did when he spoke a word and the whole universe came into existence.

So light travels 186,000 miles a second. If you do that for a

---

[3] Or just type in the address http://www.spacetelescope.org/images/opo0328a/.

year, you travel 5.88 trillion miles. A trillion is almost pointless for us to even talk about. It's beyond our ability to fully grasp. But that's a light-year, and get this: if you go twenty-nine million light-years (in the right direction!), you come to the Sombrero Galaxy. Do the math in the margin if you'd like. That's twenty-nine million (29,000,000) times 5.88 trillion miles (5,880,000,000,000).

And if you've already gone online to see the Sombrero Galaxy, you've seen how it looks so innocuous—like a Frisbee coming right at you. Some call it the flying tortilla. From our vantage point, it sits on a six-degree plain. So we get a beautiful view of it from Hubble. But don't be fooled; this galaxy is enormous in scope, and it contains an estimated two hundred billion to three hundred billion stars. And you may never even have seen it before now.

So what's it doing out there if we didn't know about it until recently? It's doing what it was made to do. It's praising God in its immensity and beauty. What a tribute to someone so amazing— even the word *amazing* seems so hollow in this case—as this God that we worship. He has a whole galaxy that is just a tiny part of the symphony of the universe that brings him praise.

WHY THE UNIVERSE IS SO BIG

A lot of astronomers are perplexed, honestly perplexed, as to why the universe is so big. It's so big that now we're spending gobs of money looking for other life forms in the universe. There is a big push right now to assume that there must be some other life forms in this mind-bogglingly massive universe. There must be more habitable planets in such vast reaches of space, they say. It's way too big, if it's just a place for you and me. To which I respond, *I totally agree.*

If the universe was created simply to house humanity, it sure seems oversized. But if these perplexed astronomers knew the right reason for the existence of the universe, they wouldn't struggle. If they knew the universe's primary function wasn't to house humanity but to magnify its Creator, then they would discover it's not too big at all. It's just about the right size to give praise to God. And that's what the heavens are doing, along with the angels, while you're reading this chapter.

Let's go to Psalm 148, and then come back to the question we're posing, *Whom shall I send?*

FROM HEAVENS TO HUMANS

Psalm 148 begins with three powerful words—"Praise the LORD!" Now you'd think, after 147 psalms, you'd have your head around that idea.[4] But the psalmist is still making the point. It seems right to have the exclamation point there. There's some horsepower in this statement. And look at what the psalmist says next:

> Praise the LORD from the heavens;
>   praise him in the heights!
> Praise him, all his angels;
>   praise him, all his hosts! (vv. 1–2)

This is the way it works with God. He likes to first remind us of things that are bigger than us (heaven, heights, angels, hosts) and then bring it down to our humble estate. Look at verses 3–6:

> Praise him, sun and moon,
>   praise him, all you shining stars!
> Praise him, you highest heavens,
>   and you waters above the heavens!
>
> Let them praise the name of the LORD!
>   For he commanded and they were created.
> And he established them forever and ever;
>   he gave a decree, and it shall not pass away.

But he doesn't want you and me to be left out of the praise. So he says, "Praise the LORD from the earth . . ." (v. 7), inviting us into his chorus—a chorus already being sung. By whom? The psalmist is not just waxing poetic when he mentions the sun and moon and

---

[4] Yes, I know the Psalms as recorded in Scripture are not chronologically sequential, but you get the point.

stars. It's not just a literary maneuver; it's really happening. In God's universe, stars don't just shine; they sing.

THE VELA PULSAR

Let me mention another star called Vela Pulsar. It's magnificent. It's a thousand light-years away. It's a highly magnetized neutron star, which simply means this star exploded into a supernova. And when it exploded, the Vela Pulsar collapsed back on itself in a magnetic entity and began oscillating on its axis. It oscillates eleven times a second on its axis. And as it oscillates, it shoots out a radio frequency. Not only do we have amazing photographs, but also, because we're determined to hear somebody out there speaking to us, we have SETI (Search for Extraterrestrial Intelligence) and other highly advanced electromagnetic telescope programs that listen to the universe day and night and pick up sounds like those from the Vela Pulsar. (When I say *we*, I mean *we* as in our tax dollars are paying large sums of money to build radio telescopes that circle the earth to continually listen to see if anybody out there is speaking to us!)

So far we haven't heard any intelligent life speaking back to us, but we do have something for our money. When we aim the radio telescopes at the Vela Pulsar, we hear an incredible rhythmic sound you can find online by Googling "hear Vela Pulsar."[5]

What does it mean? I don't know. Is that some kind of Morse Code for something? I don't know what it means, and I don't want to go too crazy here, but maybe the Vela Pulsar is acting out Psalm 148:3. "Praise him, all you shining stars!" *We're a shining star*, says Vela Pulsar. *We should praise him. Let's oscillate eleven times a second on our axis and see if we can send a radio signal into the universe that would join the rhythm section in the symphony of God's praise from all creation.* The stars are singing to him.

---

[5] Or type in the address http://www.jb.man.ac.uk/pulsar/Education/Sounds/vela.au.

47 TUC

Recently, I stumbled onto a beautiful cluster of stars called "47 Tuc." This cluster is 16,700 light-years from earth. It looks brilliant, as if God shoved thousands of diamonds together into a pile. There are a massive number of stars there. Within 47 Tuc are twenty-three millisecond pulsars, and we've recorded sixteen of them. It sounds like the string section in God's orchestra. Google "47 Tuc" and "pulsars" to listen in.[6]

GOD DRAWS US IN

When you hear the Vela Pulsar and the 47 Tuc millisecond pulsars, you hear Psalm 148 coming to life. But look at verses 7–10:

> Praise the LORD from the earth,
>   you great sea creatures and all deeps,
> fire and hail, snow and mist,
>   stormy wind fulfilling his word!
>
> Mountains and all hills,
>   fruit trees and all cedars!
> Beasts and all livestock,
>   creeping things and flying birds!

So now he's bringing us in. We've got the heavens. We have the hosts. We have the stars, the sun, the moon. And now he turns to the earth, and he names everything on the earth in some form or fashion. And then he brings in humanity.

> Kings of the earth and all peoples,
>   princes and all rulers of the earth!
> Young men and maidens together,
>   old men and children!
>
> Let them praise the name of the LORD,
>   for his name alone is exalted;
>   his majesty is above earth and heaven. (vv. 11–13)

---

[6] Or type in the address http://www.jb.man.ac.uk/~pulsar/Education/Sounds/47tuc2-8000. wav.

HERE COME THE WHALES

I love that he starts verse 7 with the great sea creatures. I was in Hawaii recently, during whale season. I was captivated by these giant beasts. They seemed like they were putting on a show for us. They would splash up and roll over and spout and blow. It was beautiful. We asked the natives, how do they get here every year? And how do they know to come to the same place to have their offspring? And how do they know how to journey? They said that the whales get around through the songs they sing. And with Psalm 148 inside of me, I said, "No kidding! I'm sure they do." So I wanted to figure out what whales sing. I did a little research and went online to find the whale songs. You can too. Take a listen for yourself. It is Psalm 148 coming to life right in front of us. That's what's happening in all creation.

Try for a moment to think what it would be like to be God, hearing praises from the stars and the whales. We tend to elevate our songs. We assume we're the only ones in the universe singing praise. I'm a songwriter, and I believe in artists, and I believe in what we do in corporate worship through song. Music is one of the expressions of our worship. But I don't think we have a clue about the other praise out there in the universe, because we don't know the expanse of the worship that is continually surrounding the throne of God. Our songs are fine, but God isn't banking on them. He is surrounded by a universe-wide symphony that's bigger than we know. Stars play, whales sing, birds flap their wings.

HEARING WHAT GOD HEARS

Imagine what it might sound like if just for a second you could be God and hear what he hears. First, bring in PSR BO329-54, another pulsar that sounds a little bit like a clock ticking.[7] It's only rotating one-and-a-half times per second, which is not all that much, but we need it to keep time. Then we add the Vela Pulsar and slow it down to be in sync. So far, just two pulsars.

---

[7]You can hear PSR BO329-54 at http://www.jb.man.ac.uk/pulsar/Education/Sounds/BO329.au.

Then we put the millisecond guys in there as the string section. Now bring in the whales. We have just two pulsars, and then sixteen others, and some whales, and we have something going. This is something you could sing along to.

The point is simply this: the God who created rhythmic stars and pulsars that sound like stringed instruments is a God who doesn't need anything. He honestly doesn't need any of us. He doesn't need a band. He doesn't need a song. He has a universe singing to him!

THE UNIVERSE: GOD'S SYMPHONY

God has a symphony of praise going on. Every time a rose blooms. Every time a bud pops open. Every bird's wings that flap through the sky. Every ocean wave that crashes on a rocky shore. Every snowflake that flitters its way down and lands softly, even imperceptibly to you and me, on the snowy ground. Lightning and the wind that blows through the trees. When a baby cries. When a child laughs. All of God's creation is praising him.

He is big, and he is powerful and beautiful and amazing and expansive in every way. And he is the one who is asking the question. How amazing that we have the chance to be involved in his work of redemption. He didn't ask anybody to help him make the universe. He didn't need Albert Einstein or Carl Sagan or anybody else. He said, *I know how to make the universe. Watch this.* And he didn't ask for your input or mine or anybody else's. He made it just the way he wanted it.

CREATION GONE WRONG

Scripture says that he fashioned a man out of the dust of the ground, and he breathed into him the very breath of life. And he took from him a rib and fashioned that into a woman while the man was asleep, and he awakened to a whole new life, and the whole new life was the man and the woman and God in harmony, in partnership together. And a God who didn't need anybody, who's never needed anybody—or anything, for that matter, who created everything that is in time and space from a place outside of time and space, now is in a garden with a man and a woman, and he says, "Hey, here's the new plan. I'm going to partner with you. You will be my caretakers of earth." Does that strike anybody else as crazy? Adam could have said, "Who's asking? You want us to take care of the place? Who's asking?" *I Am Who I Am is asking.*

But it went wrong, and a redemption story, which was already set in motion before the ages with the Lamb slain before the foundation of the world, continued, as an animal was slain as a token of God's coming sacrifice. And even in that, God partnered with us. You might say, "No, God accomplished our salvation all by himself." Yes, it's true, Jesus died alone. And he didn't get any help from any of us to be raised from the dead. Yet God included people in the process of redemption. Prophets proclaimed the way. A baby needed a parent. Even soldiers, in God's time, carried out the execution. Certainly, Jesus was born to die alone—because he was sinless and the only one who could die for our sins. None of us could be a part of that. But in his resurrection, he said partnership is still very much alive, and we are to be those proclaiming life and grace and the possibility of peace with God to all the people on the planet. *I'm choosing you*, he says, *to help finish the job in the strength I supply.*

WE HAVE A PART TO PLAY

I love the way Paul writes about this in the opening lines in the book of Romans. He unfolds the beauty of this partnership. He doesn't say it's an equal partnership, but Paul clearly has a part to play:

> Paul, a servant of Christ Jesus, called to be an apostle, set apart for the gospel of God, which he promised beforehand through his prophets in the holy Scriptures, concerning his Son, who was descended from David according to the flesh and who was declared to be the Son of God in power according to the Spirit of holiness by his resurrection from the dead, Jesus Christ our Lord. (Rom. 1:1–4)

There has been an amazing work. Christ has come to us. Grace has come to us, and with grace came a calling of apostleship on Paul's life that is fulfilled in bringing about the obedience of faith for the sake of God's name among all the nations. So there is no dividing line—no separation of mission and redemption. Inherent in our being redeemed is that we are now a part of God's redemption plan.

THE COMMISSION THAT CANNOT FAIL

The Great Commission shouldn't land on us as if Jesus is merely saying, "I want you to *go* do this." The Commission is an almost unthinkable invitation. It truly is a *Great* Commission. We have marching orders. It is clear what we Christians are to be about on this planet. There is no gray area. No haze. No mist. No need to debate or think or pray or fast for God to make himself clear on this. It is already crystal clear what the church is to be about— namely, taking the gospel of Jesus to every distinct grouping of people on planet earth at all costs for the sake of his name. But it's not as if God is throwing a manual in our laps, saying, "Go do it." Rather, it's God, who doesn't need to, choosing to invite us into his glorious plan.

God is on the move. He's going to do it. What does he promise in Psalm 46 after that memorable line, "Be still, and know that I am God"? He promises, "I will be exalted among the nations" (v. 10). The mission will not abort. Jesus promises in Matthew 24:14, "This gospel of the kingdom will be proclaimed throughout the whole world as a testimony to all nations, and then the end will come."

You or I can bail, but the mission is still going to go forward. So it's not God throwing a blueprint in our laps and saying, "Go do it." It's God saying, "This is what I'm doing. I don't know what you're doing, but this is what I'm doing. It's spectacular, and you're invited to come along and be a part of what I'm doing." He's inviting us. He's not pushing us out the door and saying, "Go do that."

He's saying, "This is what I'm doing. This is where I'm going. This is what's on my heart. Join me."

HOW TO BE CLOSE TO JESUS

If you want to be close to Jesus—and maybe you haven't felt very close to him lately—if you want to dwell intimately with the Son of God and feel the breath of heaven on your life, then you need to be where Jesus is. Perhaps you have spent way too long trying to get Jesus where you are. What you need to do is start getting onboard with the idea of getting where he is. And I'm telling you where he is: going to all the unreached peoples of the earth. That's where Jesus is. If you haven't felt a real intimacy with Christ and closeness with the Holy Spirit, it may be because you're off doing your thing, and God is elsewhere doing his thing. He's not responding to all your invitations to come over and join up with your thing. Now it's finally time for you to respond to his invitation to join up with his thing.

A couple of things happen when we join his thing. First, the nations are glad because they're waiting. People, knowingly or not, are waiting to be released from hopeless and empty lives by the grace of a universe-breathing God. Second, we are happy because we're walking with Jesus, and we're experiencing the one thing that most of us want to experience more than anything else—his closeness and presence in our lives. Maybe you're reading all the right books, attending all the right things, and coming to all the right seminars. Maybe you're honing all the right theology, but it's been a long time since you tasted a dynamic, living, intimate relationship with Jesus Christ that turns you inside out on a daily basis, where you really "taste and see that the Lord is good" (Ps. 34:8). Perhaps where the road divided was with reference to the unreached people of the world and the task of finishing the mission. He walked on to the completion of his glorious plan, surrounded by the whole creation singing his praise, while you stayed where you were and sang another worship song, the one you liked the most. Over time your heart has shriveled and you feel like your faith is waning, and God is saying to you right now, "Look, there are people who are waiting for me, and you are dying and shriveling up in trivial nothings, because you've chosen to do your thing and I'm committed to doing mine."

So who's asking? The one asking is a God who doesn't need us but who's inviting us, out of kindness and generosity and love, to get onboard with the thing he's doing in the world right now, and until the end of time. He's inviting us to walk with him as we share a role in his glorious plan.

2

THE GLORY OF GOD, THE LOSTNESS OF MAN, AND THE GOSPEL OF CHRIST

David Platt

> Praise the LORD!
> Praise God in his sanctuary;
>   praise him in his mighty heavens!
> Praise him for his mighty deeds;
>   praise him according to his excellent greatness!
> Praise him with trumpet sound;
>   praise him with lute and harp!
> Praise him with tambourine and dance;
>   praise him with strings and pipe!
> Praise him with sounding cymbals;
>   praise him with loud clashing cymbals!
> Let everything that has breath praise the LORD!
>   Praise the LORD!
>
> —*Psalm 150*

There are an estimated seventeen thousand people groups on the planet, and God deserves praise from every single one of them. Yet thousands of these people groups have yet to be reached with the gospel. Hundreds of millions of men and women who have rebelled against the sovereign glory of God have never heard about the saving grace of God. So what does this mean for our lives? And what does this mean for the church?

Gospel truths permeating Isaiah 6 reveal deafening realities that compel us to lead our churches and give our lives—and lose

47

them, if necessary—for the spread of the gospel among unreached people groups. Indeed, the glory of God among the nations is not simply a reason for a conference or a book; the glory of God among the nations is the reason for which we have breath.

THE VISION OF ISAIAH 6

In the sixth chapter of Isaiah, we have the following well-known vision of God's glory, given to us from the perspective of the prophet himself:

> In the year that King Uzziah died I saw the Lord sitting upon a throne, high and lifted up; and the train of his robe filled the temple. Above him stood the seraphim. Each had six wings: with two he covered his face, and with two he covered his feet, and with two he flew. And one called to another and said:
>
> > "Holy, holy, holy is the LORD of hosts;
> > the whole earth is full of his glory!"
>
> And the foundations of the thresholds shook at the voice of him who called, and the house was filled with smoke. And I said: "Woe is me! For I am lost; for I am a man of unclean lips, and I dwell in the midst of a people of unclean lips; for my eyes have seen the King, the LORD of hosts!"
>
> Then one of the seraphim flew to me, having in his hand a burning coal that he had taken with tongs from the altar. And he touched my mouth and said: "Behold, this has touched your lips; your guilt is taken away, and your sin atoned for."
>
> And I heard the voice of the Lord saying, "Whom shall I send, and who will go for us?" Then I said, "Here am I! Send me." And he said, "Go, and say to this people:
>
> > "'Keep on hearing, but do not understand;
> > keep on seeing, but do not perceive.'
> > Make the heart of this people dull,
> >   and their ears heavy,
> >   and blind their eyes;
> > lest they see with their eyes,
> >   and hear with their ears,
> >   and understand with their hearts,

and turn and be healed."
Then I said, "How long, O Lord?"
And he said:
"Until cities lie waste
    without inhabitant,
and houses without people,
    and the land is a desolate waste,
and the LORD removes people far away,
    and the forsaken places are many in the midst of
        the land.
And though a tenth remain in it,
    it will be burned again,
like a terebinth or an oak,
    whose stump remains
    when it is felled."
The holy seed is its stump. (vv. 1–13)

This awe-inspiring narrative reveals life-altering realities that, if we really believe and actually embrace them, change the trajectory of our lives and our churches, particularly regarding our focus on those not yet reached with the gospel.

THE GLORY OF GOD

The foundational truth of Isaiah 6 is clear: we have an incomprehensibly glorious God.

King Uzziah had ruled over Judah for fifty-two years. Americans are accustomed to a president in power for four or possibly eight years, but for fifty-two years Uzziah had been the only leader the majority of God's people had ever known. For most of his reign, he had sought God and prospered. But now, after Uzziah's prideful fall and subsequent death, the people of God found themselves amidst crisis. Amidst tragedy, Isaiah was gripped by a vision of triumph. The real King was still on the throne.

Throughout history, leaders have come and leaders have gone. Kings have come and kings have gone. Presidents have come and presidents have gone—and they will all continue to go. But one King will always remain.

This King is continually surrounded by angelic attendants, seraphs, whose name means "burning ones." These angels are virtually ablaze with the adoration of God. They live and burn to worship the Holy One. Multitudes and myriads of these angels engulf his throne, all of them flaming with pure, nuclear-powered praise of God.

Consider this: while you were sleeping last night, this choir of angels was trumpeting the glory of God. When you awoke this morning, they were still singing. As you sit here reading this book, these angels are persistently shouting his praise. And when you go to bed tonight, their chorus will not stop.

What is their song selection? It is "Holy, holy, holy." It's as if the angels are pulling on the leash of language to try to find a word to express the nature of the One who is before them, and the only word that comes out is, "Holy, holy, holy."

HOLINESS IS MORE THAN PURITY

What does it mean for God to be holy? In one sense, it means that God is without error. He is perfect—period. There is nothing wrong in our God. He has never had a wrong thought. He has never done a wrong deed. He has never had a wrong motive. Everything in him is right and righteous, unadulterated and pure.

But we must be careful to think not only of purity when we think of holiness. There is a sense in which similar things could be said of the angels who are surrounding God's throne. They are not a part of sinful man or fallen angels. In a real sense, they are also without sin. So we know that God's holiness signifies more than his only being without error. For him to be holy means that he is without equal.

God says in Isaiah 40:25, "To whom then will you compare me, that I should be like him?" In other words, "Who is my equal?" He echoes this in Isaiah 45:5, declaring, "I am the LORD, and there is no other." Indeed, there is no one like our God. It is folly to compare anyone or anything to our God, for he is incomparable.

His holiness is fittingly terrifying, and his sovereignty is total.

Isaiah exclaims, "The whole earth is full of his glory." All of creation is a continual explosion of the glory of God. God is sovereign over all of nature, down to the point of bringing out the starry host one by one, and calling them each by name (Isa. 40:26).

He is sovereign over nature, and he is sovereign over nations. Isaiah 36 paints a portrait of a historical interlude in the middle of this prophetic book. The Assyrians had overtaken the northern kingdom of Israel, and they were pressing forward violently into the southern kingdom of Judah. After demolishing villages and towns, they came to Jerusalem and surrounded the holy city with 185,000 troops.

Just imagine being in Jerusalem at that moment. You have heard about the dreaded Assyrians and the destruction they've wrought. Now they are here, outside of your home, 185,000 strong. Hezekiah is telling you to trust in God, but somehow faith seems hard to find when surrounded by this potent army.

At that moment, an Assyrian commander came before God's people to taunt them. His words were clear:

> Beware lest Hezekiah mislead you by saying, "The LORD will deliver us." Has any of the gods of the nations delivered his land out of the hand of the king of Assyria? Where are the gods of Hamath and Arpad? Where are the gods of Sepharvaim? Have they delivered Samaria out of my hand? Who among all the gods of these lands have delivered their lands out of my hand, that the LORD should deliver Jerusalem out of my hand? (Isa. 36:18–20)

This confident Assyrian commander had no clue concerning the depth of his own arrogance. At this point, God entered the conversation, and his words to Assyria were even clearer:

> Whom have you mocked and reviled?
>   Against whom have you raised your voice
> and lifted your eyes to the heights?
>   Against the Holy One of Israel!
> By your servants you have mocked the Lord,
>   and you have said, With my many chariots

I have gone up the heights of the mountains,
    to the far recesses of Lebanon,
to cut down its tallest cedars,
    its choicest cypresses,
to come to its remotest height,
    its most fruitful forest.
I dug wells
    and drank waters,
to dry up with the sole of my foot
    all the streams of Egypt.
Have you not heard
    that I determined it long ago?
I planned from days of old
    what now I bring to pass,
that you should make fortified cities
    crash into heaps of ruins,
while their inhabitants, shorn of strength,
    are dismayed and confounded,
and have become like plants of the field
    and like tender grass,
like grass on the housetops,
    blighted before it is grown.
I know your sitting down
    and your going out and coming in,
    and your raging against me.
Because you have raged against me
    and your complacency has come to my ears,
I will put my hook in your nose
    and my bit in your mouth,
and I will turn you back on the way
    by which you came. (Isa. 37:23–29)

Not long thereafter, the Lord backed up his word with his wrath:

Therefore thus says the LORD concerning the king of Assyria:
"He shall not come into this city or shoot an arrow there or come
before it with a shield or cast up a siege mound against it. By the
way that he came, by the same he shall return, and he shall not
come into this city, declares the LORD. For I will defend this city
to save it, for my own sake and for the sake of my servant David."

And the angel of the LORD went out and struck down a hundred and eighty-five thousand in the camp of the Assyrians. And when people arose early in the morning, behold, these were all dead bodies.

Then Sennacherib king of Assyria departed [as well he should] and returned home and lived at Nineveh. And as he was worshiping in the house of Nisroch his god, Adrammelech and Sharezer, his sons, struck him down with the sword. (Isa. 37:33–38)

In this brief yet devastating narrative, God clearly established that Assyria was in his hands. Babylon was in his hands. Israel and Judah were in his hands. Indeed, God is sovereign over all nations.

This, in and of itself, is good news. It is good news to know that Mahmoud Ahmadinejad in Iran is not sovereign over all. Benjamin Netanyahu, Hamid Karzai, and Barack Obama are not sovereign over all. The Lord our God is sovereign over every single one of these leaders, and he holds their nations in his hands.

God's holiness is terrifying, and his sovereignty is total. Let this humbling reality grip your soul: we worship an incomprehensibly great God.

THE LOSTNESS OF MAN

So what was Isaiah's response to the glory of this God? His reaction was not, "Wow," but, "Woe." "Woe is me! For I am lost" (Isa. 6:5). Why would he say that?

Think about the testimony of Scripture to the lostness of man. Only three chapters into the Bible, man deliberately chooses a rebellious and wayward path. Just moments after we read of unhindered communion between God and man, Adam and Eve are slandering God's goodness and spurning God's authority. "Let's eat from the tree; God doesn't know what's best for us. We know better than him. Even if God did say, 'Don't eat from the tree,' we're going to do it anyway. He's not Lord over us. We can do what we want."

Keep in mind that this is the God who beckons storm clouds, and they come. This is the God who says to the wind and to the rain, "You blow there, and you fall here," and they do it. This is the God who says to mountains, "You go here," and to the seas, "You stop there," and they obey. Everything in creation responds to the bidding of the Creator until you get to man, and you and I have the audacity to look at him and say no!

We slander God's goodness, spurn God's authority, and question God's Word. The tempter in Genesis 3 ushers sin into the world with the provocatively perilous question, "Did God really say . . . ?" Oh, it is a dangerous thing to subject God's word to man's judgment. Here in Genesis 3, man discounts divine truth with misplaced confidence in human thought.

One of the most tragic chapters in all of Scripture, Genesis 3, ripples throughout the rest of the Bible. From one man's sin comes condemnation for all men (Rom. 5:12, 18), and the portrait of man's lostness pervades every page of Scripture. We are cast out from God's favorable presence (Genesis 3). We are alienated from God and hostile toward him (Col. 1:21). We are cut off from God (Rom. 11:22), condemned by God (Rom. 5:10), and at enmity with God (James 4:4). We are separated from Christ (Eph. 2:12). We are slaves to sin (John 8:34) and dominated by Satan (2 Tim. 2:26). We are children of wrath (Eph. 2:3) and lovers of darkness (John 3:20) who have been darkened in our understanding (Eph. 4:18). We live in impurity and lawlessness (Rom. 6:19).

The lostness of man affects each of us individually and all of us collectively. Our minds are depraved. Romans 1:21–23 makes clear that our claims to be wise are full of foolishness, for we have exchanged "the glory of the immortal God for images resembling mortal man and birds and animals and creeping things." Our minds are debased (Rom. 1:28), blinded to truth by the god of this world (2 Cor. 4:4). Our emotions are disordered. Our hearts are sinful (Rom. 1:26) and the wicked passions of our flesh wage war against our souls (1 Pet. 2:11). Our minds are depraved, our emotions are disordered, and our bodies are defiled. We degrade our bodies with one another (Rom. 1:24). Hear the humbling testimony of Paul in Romans 3:10–18 as he draws upon Old Testament truth:

> None is righteous, no, not one;
>   no one understands;
>   no one seeks for God.
> All have turned aside; together they have become worthless;
>   no one does good,
>   not even one.
> Their throat is an open grave;
>   they use their tongues to deceive.
> The venom of asps is under their lips.
>   Their mouth is full of curses and bitterness.
> Their feet are swift to shed blood;
>   in their paths are ruin and misery,
> and the way of peace they have not known.
> There is no fear of God before their eyes.

In our lostness, we are morally evil. The start of Scripture describes how every inclination of our hearts is evil from childhood (Gen. 8:21). According to Jesus, we are spiritually sick (Matt. 19:12). In the end, we are all continually perishing (1 Cor. 1:18; 2 Cor. 4:3; 2 Thess. 2:9).

Do we realize all of this? Our problem is not simply that we have made some bad decisions. Our problem is not just that we've messed up. Our problem is that we are—at the very core of our being—sinfully lost, cut off from God, condemned by God, and consequently destined for hell.

Our sin before an infinitely holy God warrants infinitely horrifying judgment. This is the clear truth of all Scripture. Scottish professor James Denney once said, "If there is any Scripture at all, this is true—that those who stubbornly refuse to submit to the gospel, and to love and obey Jesus Christ, incur at the Last Advent an infinite and irreparable loss. They will pass into a night on which no morning dawns."[1]

[1] James Denney and Alexander Maclaren, *The Epistles of St. Paul to the Colossians and Philemon*, Expositor's Bible, vol. 31 (New York: Armstrong, 1905), 300.

We say things like, "We had a hell of a time." Or, "We played a hell of a game." Or, "That was a hell of a song." The way we talk about hell shows that we have no idea what we are talking about.

Hell is a place of fiery agony. Hear Jesus in Mark 9:43–48: "If your hand causes you to sin, cut it off. It is better for you to enter life crippled than with two hands to go to hell, to the unquenchable fire. . . . And if your eye causes you to sin, tear it out. It is better for you to enter the kingdom of God with one eye than with two eyes to be thrown into hell, 'where their worm does not die and the fire is not quenched.'" In the words of Revelation 20:15, "If anyone's name was not found written in the book of life, he was thrown into the lake of fire." Similarly, Revelation 21:8 envisions hell as "the lake that burns with fire and sulfur."

You say, "Well, isn't fire just an image in these passages? Aren't these verses symbolic?"

Maybe. But if they are symbols, what are they symbols for? A wintry retreat or a summer vacation? No, these are symbols that stand for something much worse. Surely burning fire and smoking sulfur are not symbols for a nice place to be. They are symbols for a terrifying place to be.

Hell is a place of conscious torment (Luke 16:22). It is a place of outer darkness (Matt. 22:13). It is a place of divine destruction where people are separated from the presence of the Lord and the power of his might (2 Thess. 1:9). And most horrifying of all, hell is a place of eternal duration.

John writes about the unbelieving being punished in hell in Revelation 14:11, saying, "The smoke of their torment goes up forever and ever." Thomas Watson said, "The wicked in hell shall be always dying but never dead; the smoke of the furnace ascends for ever and ever. Oh! who can endure thus to be ever upon the rack? The word 'ever' breaks the heart."[2] Listeners of George Whitefield were "urged to consider the torment of burning like a livid coal, not for an instant or for a day, but for millions and millions of ages,

---

[2]Thomas Watson, quoted in *The Golden Treasury of Puritan Quotations*, comp. I. D. E. Thomas (Chicago: Moody, 1975), 137.

at the end of which they would realize that they are no closer to the end than when they first begun, and they will never, ever be delivered from that place."[3]

Oh, who of us can even begin to grasp the everlasting horror of hell? We are not just playing games here. There is real, everlasting wrath awaiting lost sinners before a holy God. We cannot be ignorant of this, and we must not be indifferent to this. We must refuse to be numbed by the temporary pleasures of this world in a way that prevents us from feeling the eternal weight of heaven and hell.

This is why Isaiah said, "Woe is me, for I am lost." His lostness is not his own. It is shared by all humanity, including hundreds of millions of unreached men and women. They—and we—are sinfully lost apart from Christ. Cut off from God, condemned by God, enemies of God, slaves to sin, dominated by Satan, children of wrath, lovers of darkness, with depraved minds and disordered emotions and defiled bodies, morally evil, spiritually sick, continually perishing, and destined to hell. This is the condition of man before God.

THE GOSPEL OF CHRIST

God is incomprehensibly glorious, and man is sinfully lost. The stage is thus set for good news as Isaiah cries out in depravity, and the Lord responds in mercy.

God commands the seraphs to take a live coal from the altar and touch Isaiah's lips, and then he says these words: "Behold . . . your guilt is taken away, and your sin atoned for" (Isa. 6:7). Consider the scandal of such a statement. Isaiah is guilty. He is a responsible sinner in the presence of a righteous God. How, then, is it possible for this holy God (who does everything right and is in all ways just) to look at a guilty sinner and declare, "You are innocent"? No matter who we are—whether we're conservative, progressive, or liberal, or carry some other label—we have a sense of

---

[3] Richard Hofstadter, *America at 1750: A Social Portrait*, Vintage International Vintage Series, (New York: Vintage, 1973), 240.

right and wrong. We expect right to be praised, we expect wrong to be condemned, and we expect God to do the same. So how can God, in his perfection, look at that which is totally rebellious and say, "You are perfectly righteous"?

This is where Isaiah 6 doesn't give us the complete story. We need to travel over to Isaiah 53 to see the continuation of this portrait of a God who takes the altar of sacrifice and turns it into a place of salvation. It's a picture that God had set up among his people for generations through offerings, feasts, celebrations, and special days.

Remember the Passover. Families would take a lamb into their homes and then slaughter it only days later. They would take its blood and put it over their doorposts to show that the price for sin had been paid—death.

Fast-forward to the Day of Atonement and you see two offerings. One is sacrificed, its blood sprinkled over the atonement cover to show that the penalty of sin—death—had been doled out. Then the priest would take the other sacrifice, the scapegoat, and place his hands on the goat's head to symbolically show the passing of sin from the people onto the goat. After the priest confessed the people's sins, the sacrificial goat was taken into the wilderness, outside the camp, never to return again. It was a picture of God removing sins—taking sins away—and the same Hebrew word that is used in Leviticus 16:22 ("the goat shall *bear*") is used in Isaiah 53:4–6 ("he has *borne* our griefs") to describe what Christ the Servant will do for us:

> Surely he has borne our griefs
>   and carried our sorrows;
> yet we esteemed him stricken,
>   smitten by God, and afflicted.
> But he was pierced for our transgressions;
>   he was crushed for our iniquities;
> upon him was the chastisement that brought us peace,
>   and with his wounds we are healed.
> All we like sheep have gone astray;
>   we have turned—every one—to his own way;

and the LORD has laid on him
the iniquity of us all.

In this sobering prophecy of a suffering servant, we discover that Christ will endure the penalty of sin. All the physical suffering we see on the cross is a visible demonstration of the penalty for sin.

But that is not all. The servant will not only endure the penalty of sin; the servant will stand in the place of sinners. Isaiah draws *us* into this passage by repeatedly using the first-person plural pronoun. No less than ten times in three verses, we see what Jesus will do in *our* place—in *our* stead. "Surely he has borne *our* griefs and carried *our* sorrows. *We* esteemed him stricken. He was pierced for *our* transgressions. Crushed for *our* iniquities. Upon him was the chastisement that brought *us* peace, and with his wounds *we* are healed. All *we* like sheep have gone astray; *we* have turned every one to his own way; and the LORD has laid on him the iniquity of *us* all."

DOES GOD HATE SINNERS?

Not long ago, I wrote a book called *Radical* that attracted publicity in a variety of different places. In one local news article, a *Birmingham News* reporter took a quote from the book and wrote: "While it's a common pulpit truism that God hates sin but loves the sinner, Platt argues that God hates sinners." Indeed, it was a direct quote taken from the book, but the article obviously included no context from which the quote was taken. So church members started e-mailing me, asking, "Pastor, do you believe that God hates sinners?" People in the city e-mailed me, not so kindly, saying, "You're preaching hatred in that church and all over our city." This is one of those places where I found myself in a bit of trouble for quoting the Bible.

Does God hate sinners? Look closely at Psalm 5:5–6: "The boastful shall not stand before your eyes; you hate all evildoers. You destroy those who speak lies; the LORD abhors the bloodthirsty and deceitful man."

And this is not an isolated statement in Scripture. Fourteen times in the first fifty psalms alone, we see God's hatred toward the sinner, his wrath toward the liar, and so on. The Old Testament does not stand alone here. In John 3—that chapter where we have one of the most famous verses about God's love—we also have one of the most neglected verses about God's wrath (John 3:36).

All of this begs the question: Is it true that God hates the sin but loves the sinner?

Well, yes, of course, in one sense. But not completely. Think about it.

When we see God's holy hatred of sin and God's righteous wrath upon sin, this sin is not something outside of us. We have a tendency to think that when Jesus went to the cross, he died for our lusting, our lying, our cheating, and our doing this or that, as if our sin is outside of us. But sin is not outside of us; it is at the core of who we are. When Jesus went to the cross, he wasn't just enduring the penalty of sin; he was standing in the place of sinners. When he was crushed and bruised and literally pulverized under the weight of God's wrath, Isaiah 53 says he was doing this in our place. He was taking the full payment due you and me as sinners. In this way, we must be careful not to lean on comfortable clichés in Christianity that may rob the cross of its meaning.

The startling reality is clear: we are sinners. In the words of Isaiah, "We all like sheep have gone astray." Obviously there are many preachers today who would say, "You're good. You're fine. Trust in yourself. Believe in yourself." Don't believe them. We are dumb sheep. Even the smartest, most intellectual reader of this book is a dumb sheep lost in sin and walking his own foolish way apart from Jesus. We are all sinners, and God is completely holy, possessing righteous hatred toward sin and sinners alike.

Yet God also possesses holy love toward sinners. So how can God show both holy hatred and holy love toward sinners at the same time? This is the climactic question of the Bible, and the answer is the cross. At the cross, God showed the full expression of his wrath. Look at the verbs in Isaiah. He was stricken, smitten, afflicted, wounded, crushed, and chastised.

So does God hate sinners? Yes. Look at the cross.

But does God also love sinners? Yes. Look at the cross.

God in Christ does all of this for the salvation of sinners who warrant his wrath. For every sinner who trusts in the sacrificial death and triumphant resurrection of Christ, God declares loud and clear, "Your guilt is taken away, and your sin atoned for." He remembers our sins no more (Isa. 43:25). This doesn't mean that God has amnesia. He knows everything. The beauty of the gospel is that God knows every single sinful thought and thing you and I have ever had or done, and by the grace of Jesus, the promised servant, God does not count any of those sins against us.

NO RECORD OF ANY WRONG

I heard a story once about an Englishman who bought a Rolls Royce. It had been advertised as the car that would never, ever, ever break down. So the man bought the Rolls Royce at a hefty price and was driving it one day when, to his surprise, it broke down. He was far away from town so he called and said, "Hey, you know this car that will never break down? Well, it's broken down."

Immediately, a Rolls Royce mechanic was sent via helicopter to the location where the car was broken down. The car was fixed, and the man went on his way. Naturally, the man expected to get a bill from Rolls Royce. It was clearly expensive for them to provide such service (not often does a mechanic fly to where your car is broken down!), and he wanted to get the whole ordeal behind him. So when the bill had not yet come a few weeks later, the man called Rolls Royce and said, "I'd like to go ahead and pay my bill for my broken-down car so that we can get this behind us." In turn, Rolls Royce responded by saying, "Sir, we are deeply sorry, but we have absolutely no record of anything ever having gone wrong with your car."

Consider it! For all who turn from themselves and their sin to trust in Christ as savior and king, the God of the universe looks at your life and says, "I have absolutely no record of anything ever having gone wrong in your life." In fact, because we are clothed in Christ, he says the exact opposite: "I have a record of everything having gone right in your life."

That is a scandal.

We have a scandalously merciful Savior. And if this is all true—if we have an incomprehensibly glorious God, if we are a sinfully lost people, and if we have a scandalously merciful Savior—then only one conclusion remains. Brother or sister, we have an indescribably urgent mission.

AN URGENT MISSION

Surely this God warrants more than our raising a hand and praying a prayer. Surely this God warrants more than nominal adherence, church attendance, or casual acceptance. This God warrants complete abandonment of our plans, our possessions, our hopes, our dreams, and our lives. We lay everything we have on the table before this God, and we say, "Use me—my life, my family, my church, everything I have and everything I am—for the spread of your glory and this gospel to the ends of the earth." Indeed, the only logical response to this glorious God of grace is, "Here am I. Send me."

So let us apply these truths to the unreached, moving from Isaiah 6 specifically to Romans 1. Consider over six thousand people groups comprising more than 2.5 billion people who have little to no access to the gospel. Why must we lead our churches and give our lives—even lose them, if necessary—to spread this gospel to unreached peoples? Why must we go to them with urgency? Consider three reasons.

DAMNABLE KNOWLEDGE

First, we must go with urgency because multitudes of unreached peoples have a knowledge of God that is only sufficient to damn them to hell. Romans 1:18–20 is clear:

For the wrath of God is revealed from heaven against all ungodliness and unrighteousness of men, who by their unrighteousness suppress the truth. For what can be known about God is plain to them, because God has shown it to them. For his invisible attributes, namely, his eternal power and divine nature, have been clearly perceived, ever since the creation of the world, in the things that have been made. So they are without excuse.

Every unreached person in the world—every man in an African jungle, every woman in an Asian village, every person in a forgotten tundra—all of them have a knowledge of God that exposes the lostness of their hearts. The revelation of God that they have received is sufficient to show them that God is glorious and they are guilty. And that's all they have.

You say, "Well, what happens to the innocent guy in Africa who never hears the gospel?" The answer to this question is simple. Based upon the authority of God's Word, the innocent guy in Africa who never hears the gospel will absolutely go to heaven. The only problem is that the innocent guy in Africa does not exist. If he were innocent—which is the way this question is normally phrased—why would he need the gospel? He has no sin to be saved from. However, there are no innocent people in the world waiting to hear the gospel. As we have seen, there are guilty people all over the world needing to hear the gospel, and that's why we must go to them—precisely because they are guilty. No one is innocent.

As you feel the weight of your lostness that drives you to God's grace, feel that weight for people who have enough knowledge of God to show them they are lost but nothing more. Over 2.5 billion people have just enough knowledge of God to damn them to hell.

THE GOSPEL: POWERFUL ENOUGH TO SAVE

This leads us to the second reason why we must go to the unreached: the gospel of God is powerful enough to save them for heaven. This gospel of a scandalously merciful Savior is good news for every person and every people group on the planet. And this gospel works!

Consider this true story from an impoverished area in east India. Rajesh is a pastor who lives in one of the most spiritually and physically desolate places in India—home to the poorest of the poor and only 0.01 percent evangelical. The death rate in Rajesh's area is about five thousand people per day, which means that every day 4,950 people are plunged into hell. For generations, the spiritual ground around Rajesh has been hard, and the physical poverty has been harrowing. Rajesh was at the end of his rope in his ministry, but he went to a conference on disciple making and church multiplication where he was encouraged, refreshed, and renewed.

At this conference, Rajesh was challenged to walk into a totally unreached village and say to the first person he met, "I'm here in the name of Jesus, and I would like to pray for you and your village." Rajesh rolled his eyes, thinking that would never work. But because he was at the end of his rope, he agreed to try it. He went into an unreached village, approached the first man he saw, and said, "I'm here in the name of Jesus, and I'd like to pray for you and your village."

This man replied, "I've never heard about Jesus. Can you tell me more about him?"

Surprised, Rajesh responded, "Sure."

The man said, "Wait, I want to have my friends here, too."

So Rajesh followed this guy to a home where in a matter of minutes he found himself surrounded by a group of people wanting him to tell them about Jesus. Within two weeks, twenty-five of them had placed their faith in Christ for salvation. Then those new believers decided, "Why don't we start doing the same thing that Rajesh did for us?" In the days that have followed, churches have been planted in 115 different villages in that area.

This gospel is powerful.

This is why you can go with confidence to the hardest, most difficult places and peoples on the planet. When we send people out from our church, we are sending them out with death-defying conviction that this gospel has the power to save. When we adopt a people group, we know that people group one day will be represented around the throne of Christ in Revelation 7. So no matter how challenging it may seem, we preach the gospel, knowing that someone in every people group is going to respond in faith. Indeed, there is not a people group on the planet that is beyond the power of God to save. And people who believe this cannot sit on this gospel. People who believe this will eagerly leave their comforts and gladly give their lives proclaiming this gospel among the nations.

THE GLORY OF GOD: GOOD ENOUGH TO SATISFY

We must take the gospel to unreached people groups because their knowledge of God is only enough to damn them to hell, and the gospel of God is powerful enough to save them for heaven. This leads us to the final and ultimate reason why we must take this gospel to the unreached: because the glory of God is good enough to satisfy them forever.

There is coming a day when our scandalous Savior and sovereign King will return, and he will surround himself with a throng from every people group, nation, tribe, and tongue. We will see his face, and together we will be glad in his glory. This is the definitive reason why we rise and say without condition and regardless of cost, "Here we are, Lord, send us." This is what we live for. This is what we die for. Indeed, this is why we have breath.

3

CHRIST, COURAGE, AND FINISHING THE MISSION

Michael Ramsden

And what more shall I say? For time would fail me to tell of Gideon, Barak, Samson, Jephthah, of David and Samuel and the prophets—who through faith conquered kingdoms, enforced justice, obtained promises, stopped the mouths of lions, quenched the power of fire, escaped the edge of the sword, were made strong out of weakness, became mighty in war, put foreign armies to flight. Women received back their dead by resurrection. Some were tortured, refusing to accept release, so that they might rise again to a better life. Others suffered mocking and flogging, and even chains and imprisonment. They were stoned, they were sawn in two, they were killed with the sword. They went about in skins of sheep and goats, destitute, afflicted, mistreated—of whom the world was not worthy wandering about in deserts and mountains, and in dens and caves of the earth. And all these, though commended through their faith, did not receive what was promised, since God had provided something better for us, that apart from us they should not be made perfect. Therefore, since we are surrounded by so great a cloud of witnesses, let us also lay aside every weight, and sin which clings so closely, and let us run with endurance the race that is set before us, looking to Jesus, the founder and perfecter of our faith, who for the joy that was set before him endured the cross, despising the shame, and is seated at the right hand of the throne of God.

—*Hebrews 11:32–12:2*

We live at a time in the West in which we find it hard to imagine the scenes described in Hebrews 11:32–40. Yet if we were to talk to some of our brothers and sisters from around the world, not only would we discover that they can they imagine such things but also that they have seen, witnessed, and in some cases even experienced these things. Ours is not a peaceful world.

Just recently I received the following e-mail:

Dear friends,
Greetings. It is with great sadness that I am sharing this news with you. On the evening of June 21, a group of Christians was worshiping in a house in Peshawar, NWFP, when terrorists came on two trucks and kidnapped 32 worshipers [at] gunpoint. Police [have] confirmed the news. Christians have been taken to the Tribal area. Christians from Charsada, Mardan, and Peshawar had been receiving threatening letters from the extremists to convert to Islam, leave or be killed. It is a very dangerous situation. Please pray for their safe return.

If this were an isolated incident, the church would rise in prayer and support, and respond. Yet there are so many incidents that we can become numb to them, indifferent, or, perhaps even worse, we simply ignore them for fear that the fact that such things happen could lead us to doubt a God of love. Yet Jesus, in preparing his disciples for the trials of this world, told them that difficulty would come. They might have thought that with God on their side, no suffering would ever befall them. Jesus, however, told them:

I have said all these things to you to keep you from falling away. They will put you out of the synagogues. Indeed, the hour is coming when whoever kills you will think that he is offering service to God. (John 16:1–2)

A COSTLY CALLING

Immediately before uttering these words Jesus said, "And you also will bear witness . . ." (John 15:27)—and this word *witness* translates the Greek word *martys*, from which we have the contemporary word *martyr.* So how did a word that simply meant "witness" come to be so closely identified with suffering, persecution, and even death?

Negatively, the word *martyr* can mean to be driven by an "exaggerated desire to sacrifice oneself for others and have the sacrifice recognized by others."[1] The biblical use and historical development of the word, however, is not about recognition of a sacrifice made by us but rather a willingness to suffer in order to properly recognize and proclaim the sacrifice made by Jesus. In being a faithful witness to Jesus, we are promised that persecution *will* come—"If they persecuted me, they will also persecute you" (John 15:20). "The world hated me," Jesus said in John 15:18, and so we should not be surprised at the hatred that we ourselves attract on account of his name (John 15:21).

We read in Hebrews that faith and faithfulness lead both to great victories in his name—kingdoms were conquered, justice was enforced, promises were obtained, mouths of lions were stopped, the power of fire was quenched, the edge of the sword was escaped from, foreign armies were put to flight, and women received back their dead by resurrection—*and* also to great cost, as the world would see it—some were tortured, and others suffered mocking, flogging, chains, and imprisonment. They were stoned, they were sawn in two, they were killed with the sword. Truly they were those of whom the world was not worthy.

So let us set aside any thoughts we may have about being able to witness without cost. There are both great miracles (escaping the sword) and great martyrdoms (many were killed by the sword). There is no contradiction here—just the certain knowledge that we are called to give our lives in his service and will one day be called home.

This is not a unique time in history. There is always a cost to reaching people with the good news about Jesus. It is a cost that perhaps many who identify with Jesus may not ultimately be prepared to pay. But this is the context within which the gospel took root and spread. Preaching a message of repentance and faith has always been challenging. It has always required courage. I have had the privilege of speaking in some parts of the world in which personal safety cannot be guaranteed. It is always disap-

---

[1] *Oxford English Dictionary*, 2nd ed., s.v. "martyr."

pointing when some express concerns that maybe I shouldn't go to a particular place because the risks are too great. Our goal is not to conserve our lives at any cost but rather to live our life in obedience to the call we have received. We are not called to ignore risk or to be reckless. Everything must be prayerfully considered. But to refuse God's call to go because of hardship is to demand something that the apostles would struggle to recognize as part of genuine Christian obedience.

We follow in the footsteps of the "martyrs," the witnesses, who went before us. They were not spectators wishing to be entertained. They went ahead of us and ran the race well. They are not few in number; they are a great cloud. The stands they occupy are not sparsely filled—they are packed—with those who laid down their lives in service to him who is the author of life itself, and who now have eternal life through the founder and perfecter of that faith. We are surrounded by so great a cloud of witnesses, we read in Hebrews 12:1, so let us not lose heart, or lose our way, but, rather, fixing our eyes on Christ, let us run after him who despised the shame of the cross and is now seated at the right hand of God. Let us fix our eyes on things above and go to the nations.

That said, it seems that a courageous determination to finish the mission Jesus has given us is waning. Let me make just two observations that I believe are a part of this.

1) A LOSS OF CONVICTION

It is very hard to give your life to something that you believe is not true. It is entirely possible to act out of mistaken conviction (you believe something to be true when actually it is false). But it is very unlikely that you will act at all if you have come to the conclusion that what you believe is actually false. The Christian worldview is under attack from many different quarters, and some have come to feel that there is no response to these critiques. But if the Christian faith is not true, if we have followed cleverly invented stories, why bother suffering in relation to it?

You may prefer Hans Christian Andersen's versions of the classic fairy tales to the earlier versions, but would you lay down your life in defense of this preference for a collection of stories that aren't real?

Defeated by Philosophy?

There are two basic objections that many seem to wrestle with. The first is philosophical in nature—that, by definition, since Christianity is a faith, it is not concerned with either truth or reality. If that is the case, then it is not really capable of being either true or false, but only of being believed by virtue of faith or ignored by virtue of reason. This would make the gospel a matter of private preference (simply what one would like to be true) rather than public conviction (what is true even if you would prefer to ignore it).

Yet this is manifestly not what is meant by faith. Rather than faith being belief by speculation, the biblical term *pistis* (faith) carries with it the act of trusting in that which is true and real and has quite strong moral connotations. In this sense, we still use the biblical word *faith* even today. When I say, "I have faith in the American government," I am saying two things. First, I am saying that there is such a thing as the American government. Its existence is not a matter of personal preference—even if you didn't want it to exist, it wouldn't make any difference to the fact that it does. Second, I am saying that I believe those in government are trustworthy, that they are true to their word. If they make a promise, I can count on it. If that promise is broken, the result will be disillusionment born out of a sense of betrayal (they promised one thing and did another). In other words, they were not true to their word. My faith, what I trust in, is in response to that which I believe is true and real.

This is the overriding sense of the word in the New Testament. Earlier in the book of Hebrews, we are told that "without faith it is impossible to please him, for whoever would draw near to God must believe that he exists and that he rewards those who seek him" (Heb. 11:6). This tells us two things about the faith that pleases God; namely, that it is connected to reality (he exists) and that he is trustworthy (he rewards those who seek him—he is true to his word). Hence, the hope that comes from God does not disappoint. It is real and is shown to be real in times of trial, and God is true to his word; he is trustworthy.

Faith is not strengthened by distancing ourselves from reality and truth; this would make faith psychological and dependent on our ability to generate it. Rather, faith is the only legitimate response to the God who is both true and real. This is why Christians have always been concerned about the historicity and reality of the cross and resurrection and also concerned with consistency and fulfillment of his word.

We have put our faith, our trust, in Christ. Our faith does not make Christ's existence possible. It is because of Christ's reality that our faith is real, and on that basis, we know that the things we now hope for are sure, and the things we do not yet see are bound to pass because of the one who has promised them. We can be confident at the bar of truth.

Subdued by Science?

The second fear stems from science, that in a scientific world the claims of Christ are neither credible nor compatible with a scientific worldview.[2] Let me address just two particular issues that seem to keep Christians quiet about their faith.

First, there is the fear that as our scientific understanding of the world grows in terms of both scope and depth, the shady areas occupied by God are being rapidly diminished by the light of science. The "god of the gaps" is literally, therefore, being made homeless; there are no gaps left for him to live in or occupy. However, the God of Scripture is not the god of the gaps.

Stephen Hawking, one of the world's most famous scientists, recently announced that our understanding of the universe is

---

[2] I would recommend generally looking at the works of John Lennox, professor of mathematics at the University of Oxford, and of professor Alister McGrath.

such that God is no longer needed to be seen as the creator of the universe; we now understand the laws by which the universe came into being.[3] But this makes a serious philosophical mistake, confusing the categories of law and agency.

My house in Oxford is not of a complicated design. It was built around 1880 and shares its name with a missionary hospital established in London at about the same time. Its architecture, the physics and mathematics behind why it is still standing, the materials of which it is composed, and so on are exhaustively described by science. There are no gaps in our understanding of it. Does that mean we can conclude that there is no designer? No architect? This would be to confuse the categories of law and agency. Even if we have an exhaustive understanding of the laws of science, that would not be philosophically capable of disproving whether there was an agent, God, behind it all. The argument cannot be made to work. Let us not fear science, therefore; it can only add to our sense of wonder of the world in which we live.

The second general struggle comes from the fact that God, in general, and the miraculous, in particular, are unscientific in that they violate the laws of nature, and hence God either doesn't exist or cannot act.

Imagine, however, that you took this book that you are now holding and threw it across the room. If I knew certain facts, such as the angle of departure and the velocity, then I could predict, with great accuracy, its flight path and where it will land. There is nothing mysterious about it. However, let us imagine that, having thrown the book, it were to come to rest midair. Is this a violation of the law of gravity? No, it is not. The law of gravity is still very much in play. But either something (that I cannot see) or someone (whom I cannot see) is holding it there. It is because we live in a universe governed by mathematical law and physics

---

[3] He posed the question: "Is the way the universe began chosen by God for reasons we can't understand, or was it determined by a law of science? I believe the second. If you like, you can call the laws of science 'God,' but it wouldn't be a personal God that you could meet, and ask questions." *Daily Telegraph*, September 2, 2010.

that I am able to come to that conclusion. If the universe we live in were not governed by such fixed laws, we would not be able to reliably detect the intervention of anyone or any force in any course of events.

God has established a world in which his miraculous intervention can be detected and in which science is possible. But to claim that God could not exist, or that you could not believe in him, because God's intervention violates scientific law would be, therefore, impossible. C. S. Lewis puts it the following way:

> If this week I put a thousand pounds in the drawer of my desk, add two thousand next week and another thousand the week thereafter, the laws of arithmetic allow me to predict that the next time I come to my drawer, I shall find four thousand pounds. But suppose when I open the drawer, I find only one thousand pounds, what shall I conclude? That the laws of arithmetic have been broken? Certainly not! I might reasonably conclude that some thief has broken the laws of the State and stolen three thousand pounds out of my drawer. One thing that would be ludicrous to claim is that the laws of arithmetic make it impossible to believe in the existence of such a thief or the possibility of his intervention. On the contrary, it is the normal workings of those laws that have exposed the existence and activity of the thief.[4]

There is nothing in science, or in philosophy, that should lead us to conclude that our convictions are neither true nor real. Rather, let us be prepared to give answers to those who ask us for the reason for the hope that we have and make sure that we do it with gentleness and respect (1 Pet. 3:15–16). Silence is not an option when faced with hard questions from these disciplines, and, as a church, we desperately need to regain our public voice and proclaim the gospel to a world desperately in need.

2) A MARRIAGE OF CONVENIENCE

There is another criticism that is leveled at Christians, however, and I take it much more seriously. It has been most eloquently

---

[4]C. S. Lewis, *Miracles* (Oxford, UK: Lion, 2009), 200.

put by Professor John Gray, former professor of European thought at the London School for Economics. In his book *Straw Dogs*, he launches a sustained attack on humanism from his convictions as a serious atheist. From there, he goes on to argue that morality is a convenience, a Christian myth. The initial conclusions he comes to, however, are so important to our theme that I would like to take the time to allow him to build his case, and I will try to summarize it using largely his own words.

John Gray correctly states that in the West, we live in a Humanistic world. I capitalize it because it is the dominant ideology. Gray calls it a religion[5]:

> Humanism is not science, but religion—the post-Christian faith that humans can make a world better than any in which they have so far lived.[6]

However, he says, the truly secular view of the world is one that doesn't intellectually permit the belief in, or hopes of, Humanism. As he says, "A truly naturalistic view of the world leaves no room for secular hope."[7] The problem with Humanism, he argues, is not its atheism and its Darwinian roots but that it has not been true to those roots. Humanism, he argues, has actually been taken captive by the Christianity that came before it. Humanism is simply Christianity in a secular form, which has replaced the idea of God's providence with that of progress. He writes:

> Christians understood history as a story of sin and redemption. Humanism is the transformation of this Christian doctrine of salvation into a project of universal emancipation. The idea of progress is a secular version of the Christian belief in providence. . . .
> The idea of progress rests on the belief that the growth of knowledge and the advance of the species go together—if not now, then in the long run.[8]

---

[5] John Gray, *Straw Dogs: Thoughts on Humans and Other Animals* (London: Granta, 2004).
[6] Ibid., *xiii*.
[7] Ibid., *xii*.
[8] Ibid., *xiii–xiv*.

However, he immediately goes on to say:

> The biblical myth of the Fall of Man contains the forbidden truth.
> Knowledge does not make us free. It leaves us as we have always
> been, prey to every kind of folly.[9]

So, he argues that the idea that we are fallen is actually
closer to human nature than the utopian view of man advocated
by Humanism. This being the case, however, he argues that the
conviction that "progress" will make us better is wrong.

> To believe in progress is to believe that, by using the new powers
> given us by growing scientific knowledge, humans can free them-
> selves from the limits that frame the lives of other animals. . . .
> Darwin showed that humans are like other animals, humanists
> claim they are not. Humanists insist that by using our knowl-
> edge we can control our environment and flourish as never before.
> In affirming this, they renew one of Christianity's most dubious
> promises—that salvation is open to all. The humanist belief in
> progress is only a secular version of this Christian faith. In the
> world shown us by Darwin, there is nothing that can be called
> progress.
>   The idea of humanity taking charge of its destiny makes
> sense only if we ascribe consciousness and purpose to the spe-
> cies; but Darwin's discovery was that species are only currents
> in the drift of genes. The idea that humanity can shape its future
> assumes that it is exempt from this truth.[10]

Of course, there is then a problem with the notion of truth itself.

> Modern humanism is the faith that through science humankind
> can know the truth—and so be set free. But if Darwin's theory
> of natural selection is true this is impossible. The human mind
> serves evolutionary success, not truth. To think otherwise is to
> resurrect the pre-Darwinian error that humans are different
> from all other animals. . . .

---

[9] Ibid., *xiv*.
[10] Ibid., 4.

Darwinian theory tells us that an interest in truth is not needed for survival or reproduction. More often it is a disadvantage. Deception is common among primates and birds. . . .

Truth has no systematic evolutionary advantage over error. Quite to the contrary, evolution will select for a degree of self-deception, rendering some facts and motives unconscious so as not to betray—by the subtle signs of self-knowledge—the deception being practiced. . . . In the struggle for life, a taste for truth is a luxury—or else a disability.[11]

The problem, Gray argues, is that though philosophers have shaken off Christianity, they have not "given up Christianity's cardinal error." What is that error? It is "the belief that humans are radically different from all other animals." We are not different. Darwin, Gray says, shows that we are animals just like any other. There is nothing special about us, but we have deceived ourselves into thinking that we are special.

If it is granted that mankind was not created in God's image (because there is no God for us to be the image of), and that we are much like the animals, and that really truth is a philosophical fiction, then other things must immediately follow.

First is a collapse of meaning: "If we truly leave Christianity behind, we must give up the idea that human history has a meaning. Neither in the ancient pagan world nor in any other culture has human history ever been thought to have an overarching significance."[12]

Second, we must get away from the idea of "persons," that human beings are somehow special because they have personhood:

Among Christians the cult of personhood may be forgiven. For them, everything of value in the world emanates from a divine person, in whose image humans are made. But once we have relinquished Christianity the very idea of the person becomes suspect.[13]

---

[11] Ibid., 27.
[12] Ibid., 47.
[13] Ibid., 58.

Third, Gray says, since we are not persons, in what sense can we talk about being responsible for our actions?

Last then, this means that we must abandon the notion of morality, which he labels as an ugly superstition. He illustrates it as follows:

> Here is a true story. A sixteen-year old prisoner in a Nazi concentration camp was raped by a guard. Knowing that any prisoner who appeared without a cap on morning parade was immediately shot, the guard stole his victim's cap. The victim once shot, the rape could not be uncovered. The prisoner knew that his only chance of life was to find a cap. So he stole the cap of another inmate, asleep in bed, and lived to tell the tale. The other prisoner was shot.
>
> Roman Frister, the prisoner who stole the cap, describes the death of his fellow inmate as follows:
>
> > The officer and the kapo walked down the lines. . . . I counted the seconds as they counted the prisoners. I wanted it to be over. They were up to row four. The capless man didn't beg for his life. We all knew the rules of the game, the killers and the killed alike. There was no need for words. The shot rang out without warning. There was a short, dry, echoless thud. One bullet to the brain. They always shot you in the back of the skull. There was a war on. Ammunition had to be used sparingly. I didn't want to know who the man was. I was delighted to be alive.
>
> What does morality say the young prisoner ought to have done? It says the human life has no price. Very well. Should he therefore have consented to lose his life? Or does the pricelessness of life mean that he was justified in doing anything to save his own? Morality is supposed to be universal and categorical. But the lesson of Roman Frister's story is that it is a convenience, to be relied upon only in normal times.[14]

This is quite a narrative. If there is no God, then John Gray's conclusions seem to follow. However, two things that Gray is con-

---

[14] Ibid., 89.

vinced of—that history, including the history of Christendom, shows that morality is a convenience, and that we have a widespread belief in the idea of progress as the belief that "humanity can shape its future"—I find of particular importance.

Starting with the latter point first, I wonder to what extent we are dependent on the Father, Son, and Holy Spirit in all that we do? Are we looking for man-made solutions to spiritual problems? To what extent is it true today that what was begun in the Spirit, we are trying to finish in the flesh? Is it possible that, just as the values of Humanism are actually Christian expressed in secular terms, that Christianity has become a form of secular Humanism with a spiritual veneer?

I am reminded of a story told to me by an American friend of mine. A leader from the Chinese underground church had come and spent several months looking at "cell church" models in the West to see what he could learn and take back to China. When asked, at the end of the trip, what he had learned, he simply replied, "It is amazing how much you can do without God."

However, it is the moral observations he makes that make me really sit up and listen. We are called as Christians to pick up our cross and follow Christ. It is impossible to be a disciple of Christ without understanding this. Why is it that there is so little evidence of it?

THE CHALLENGE OF AFFLUENCE

Our affluent culture looks for ease in everything. Comfort is prized more than anything else. In his book, *The Challenge of Affluence*, Professor Avner Offer makes the observation that moral prudence is required in order to build up affluence and wealth. However, affluence gives rise to temptation. Temptation, if not morally recognized and resisted, gives rise to indulgence. Indulgence eats up wealth. Hence, the "rewards of affluence produce the disorders of affluence."[15]

Where is the church that denies itself? I am convinced that

---

[15] Avner Offer, *The Challenge of Affluence: Self-Control and Well-Being in the United States and Britain Since 1950* (Oxford, UK: Oxford University Press, 2006).

these two issues—a lack of conviction about the truth of the gospel, and our marriage of convenience to a Christian faith that will help us get ahead in the world but without any real cost—are connected. If we conclude that the gospel is not true and real at its core, then we may still decide to believe it if we think it will help us get ahead. There are very few Western politicians I can think of that haven't found it useful to court the Christian faith and the Christian community when it is convenient to them or necessary to achieve some other goal. But what about our own lives? Do we live as if our faith is "a convenience, to be relied upon only in normal times"?

A MISSION LIKE NO OTHER

There is not much more that really needs to be said about this as it pertains to our topic. If we know the truth of the gospel, if God is with us, we need not fear what might be ranged against us. Both our lives and our words will be lived without worldly fear. The affluence that the Protestant work ethic produced in society has led to an increasingly narcissistic culture as we have moved further from the gospel and its demands. It is hard to run with endurance when burdened by a lot of weight. By not laying aside every weight and sin that clings so closely, we are trying to run a marathon in heavy clothing soaked through with indulgence.

I recently had a man train with us who has spent much of his life fighting behind enemy lines in covert operations. Following his coming to Christ, he asked if he could train with us in order to travel to more challenging parts of the world and make Christ known. When I asked him what motivated his desire to train, he replied that when he worked in covert operations, regardless of the hardship, regardless of the cost, he worked in a small unity that was dedicated to achieving its goal. He went on, "Now that I have become a Christian, Christ has given me a mission that is more important than anything that any government has ever asked of me. But where is the commitment to achieve it? Where is the willingness to suffer? Many people seem to be sitting around complaining that they don't like the chairs in the sanctuary."

CHRIST-GIVEN COURAGE

The courage we need to finish our mission is not something that we can simply arouse in ourselves. Hebrews talks of those who "were made strong out of weakness" (Heb. 11:34). The implication is not that they made themselves strong, just that they made themselves available. As a result, they were made mighty. God is able to do more than we can imagine.

When we talk about courage, we often talk about it in the face of unlikely odds or in the face of the unknown. Yet Christian courage is of a slightly different order. We know what the final outcome will be. The Lamb wins. Hence why "some were tortured, refusing to accept release, so that they might rise again to a better life" (Heb. 11:35). The outcome of our own lives is unknown to us, but it is known to God. So we may have great confidence in the errands on which he sends us.

EVERYTHING TO GAIN

I do not wish to say that this is easy, but only that it is necessary. I remember speaking in a difficult situation once. Sitting only a few feet away was a man of militant disposition, who stared at me with such hatred in his eyes the whole time I was preaching of the gospel that I was scared. In the end, I had to turn my back slightly as I spoke to blank him out, so disturbing was the look on his face. I have heard the term *death stare* before. But I had never experienced anything like that before, or since. Ending my message, I went to leave from the podium to my left, bypassing him. As I did so, I felt a challenge in my own heart. I stopped and walked right instead. As I stepped down, he stood up and I greeted him. Much to my surprise he embraced me, and as tears came down his cheeks he said, "Listening to your gospel is like watching flowers grow in a barren field."

We have everything to lose by not heeding his voice to go and make disciples of all nations, and everything to gain.

4

FROM EVERY LAND TO EVERY LAND

The Lord's Purpose and Provision in the Lord's Prayer

Michael Oh

> Pray then like this:
> "Our Father in heaven,
> hallowed be your name.
> Your kingdom come,
> your will be done,
> on earth as it is in heaven.
> Give us this day our daily bread,
> and forgive us our debts,
> as we also have forgiven our debtors.
> And lead us not into temptation,
> but deliver us from evil."
>
> —*Matthew 6:9–13*

As a kid, I had an evening ritual while going to bed. I would see the poster on my wall with the Lord's Prayer on it and pray it. I'd do my thing, "Our Father, who art in heaven . . . ," and then I'd wait for blessing. I had done my duty—my incantation to the divine—and now I thought he owed me. *Definitely gonna win my ice hockey game tomorrow. Just waiting for that college acceptance letter.* The divine had been put on notice!

The Lord's Prayer is perhaps the most beautiful prayer ever prayed, but it is so often just rambled through instead of understood and embraced and *truly* prayed and *truly* lived. And as we ramble through the prayer, we miss out on the opportunity to understand not just prayer but the Lord's teaching on the purpose of life.

So allow me to pose to you a foundational question: What is the purpose of your life? What makes life worth living? One way to look at this question of what the purpose of life is and should be for the Christian is to see what Jesus taught us in how to pray. Jesus's foundational prayer reflects the foundational, essential Christian life. Let me say this again: *in Jesus's foundational, model prayer, we can find tremendous insight—perhaps even call it a summary of Jesus's teaching on the foundational, essential Christian life and purpose.*

There is a basic biblical principle that we can see a little later in Matthew 6: "For where your treasure is, there your heart will be also" (v. 21). And similarly, what you pray about and for, there your heart is also. Your prayers are a reflection of your heart. So if we want to understand the Lord's heart, the Lord's treasure, we can find it in the Lord's Prayer.

It's commonly understood that there are two parts to the Lord's Prayer, the first half being the first three petitions, and the second half being the second three petitions. I agree with the structure, but I want to make a suggestion that the two parts *relate* to each other—and I want to make a suggestion as to how the two parts relate to each other. More on that below.

So let's dig into the text.

"OUR FATHER IN HEAVEN"

First, this is a shockingly direct and personal addressing of God in prayer—as Father. And then, second, Jesus shockingly incorporates *us* into his sonship.

If there was anyone who could claim exclusive right to address God as "My Father," it was Jesus. In teaching us to pray to God as "Our Father," Jesus invites us into corporate familial identity. And *our* Father will be addressed as *my* Father by children of God from every tribe, language, people, and nation on earth.

Here we see that there is an overwhelming, undeniable otherness to God—God *in heaven.* We see that God has perspective—heavenly perspective—that we do not share. He has unbelievable reach. He has grand exaltation. He has heavenly authority.

And to this God, we, the church, the global church, are taught to pray. We can see in the first three petitions, this first half, prayers for worship, kingdom, and obedience:

- "hallowed be your name": worship
- "your kingdom come": kingdom
- "your will be done": obedience

These are three distinct, but also very much related, petitions.

"HALLOWED BE YOUR NAME"

First, worship: "Hallowed be your name." So here, purpose is now revealed. The first petition that Jesus teaches us to pray is toward the glory and worship of our heavenly Father—*Hallowed be your name!* It's the New Testament flipside of the third commandment—*May your name not be taken in vain, but instead be treated as holy!* It is the heartfelt prayer that God will be worshiped and adored. It is the prayer that our affection for God would be rivaled by no other affection. We are to pray starting on the individual level for a holy, stark, evident, undeniable contrast between the hallowing of God in our lives and the worship, adoration, or affection toward anyone or anything else.

If I could say just one word, one perfectly appropriate and fitting and glorious word of worship to my Lord for eternity—one single word to capture this worship petition—I think it might be the word *worthy.*

Though the Sanhedrin declared that Jesus was "worthy of death," each follower of Christ will one day join with the angels, ten thousand times ten thousand, in the loud and eternal song of praise: "Worthy is the Lamb who was slain, to receive power and wealth and wisdom and might and honor and glory and blessing!" (Rev. 5:12).

So individually we are to pray and live out "Hallowed be your name." But personal doxology is not enough. God's purposes are global. And God's people should have a holy dissatisfaction with the worshiplessness of the world, a holy dissatisfaction that more than two billion people in the world have little or no access to the gospel of Jesus—and those two billion do not worship or hallow the blessed and worthy name of the God who created them.

And may our passion for God's global glory be not merely in song. Today we have some praise songs that focus wonderfully on God's global glory. But if our lives don't reflect that God is worthy of global glory and worthy of our purpose and passion, we sing empty words.

Hallowed be your name—not just in song, but in life. Not just personal, but global. And not just doxological, but *petitional*. This is not just a doxological statement—"Hallowed be your name"—it is a petition. It is a cry to God to mobilize, to work in power to bring about the worship of his name.

"YOUR KINGDOM COME"

"Your kingdom come" is very much related to the first petition. As each individual hallows and worships God, the kingdom grows. As each family hallows and worships God, the kingdom grows. As each *nation* hallows and worships God, the kingdom grows. Your kingdom *come! Do it, Lord!* We can't! Help us! That is our cry. Jesus teaches us to pray kingdom-ushering, kingdom-calling prayers.

So, how far have we come toward the building of the kingdom of God? We've seen tremendous advances toward the global expansion of the kingdom of God. Christianity today is a more global faith than at any time in history. There are Christians literally in every nation on earth. There has been tremendous kingdom growth in Latin America, Africa, and Asia. Christianity is today stronger in the Southern Hemisphere than in the Northern, and stronger in the East than in the West.

This growth is part of a very important message—that Christianity is not an *American* religion, and missions is not

West to East. It is from everywhere to everywhere, reflecting both the reality of the global church and the global goal of our faith.

In the Lord's Prayer, and in the whole of the Bible, we see that God's purpose for his people, the purpose for every single Christian from every single nation, is to pray toward and pursue his global glory through the global spread and enjoyment of the gospel.

From every nation *to* every nation.

Every nation a mission-sending nation.

Every nation a part of God's global and eternal purposes.

Every church and *every* Christian a part of God's global and eternal purposes.

Today nearly 70 percent of the world's missions force is from the majority or non-Western world.[1] The gospel is going forth *from everywhere to everywhere.* Through this global mission force, evangelical Christianity is the fastest growing religion in the world today.

Christians throughout the world are reaching the lost in their own nations (which is *evangelism*) and reaching the unreached in other nations (which is *missions*).

Kingdom Come in South America and Brazil

In South America, there has been phenomenal growth of the church and passion for global missions. Brazilians are reaching their own—many of whom have not traditionally been the object of the church's love.

I have a friend in Brazil who has an outreach to transvestites in his city. I'll admit that it's quite a nontraditional outreach. They actually hold beauty pageants to gather and connect with these transvestites. And the prize for the winner is . . . a Bible! And they've seen the power of the gospel transform the lives of former transvestites.

Brazilian churches are also reaching the nations by sending

---

[1] Jason Mandryk, State of the World address, Lausanne Younger Leaders Gathering, 2006.

out more than two thousand missionaries to reach the unreached. Brazilian churches, the first that I had heard of, were investing 75 percent of their church budgets in global missions.

Thank you, my Brazilian brothers and sisters, for your passion for the kingdom of God.

Kingdom Come in Asia

God is doing amazing things in and through Asians—reaching their own and reaching the world.

In 1951, when Communists took over China, the largest InterVarsity-related student ministry in the world was in China—one in every eighteen students was involved in Chinese InterVarsity groups. Despite the takeover, the Communists allowed the Christian groups to continue for two years after the political changes, but they placed spies in many of the groups. The fellowship in Shanghai was particularly large, so the government made sure to place a spy to observe and report on the group. Within one year, that spy became a follower of Jesus. Everyone knew he was a spy during that time, but they loved him. So when he was asked, "What contributed to your conversion experience?" he said, "You loved me too much, even though you knew I was a spy. I found your love irresistible!"[2]

Conservatively, there are today seventy-five million Christians in China.

There were less than twenty thousand Christians in Korea 110 years ago. Today South Korea has sent out more than 21,500 missionaries to 175 nations. South Korea today is very likely the primary mission-sending nation in the world. To my Korean brothers and sisters, I do have one word of challenge, however. Be careful of any pride in your hearts. I think if John the Baptist had been Korean, he would have made Jesus call him "Hyung Nim," or "honored older brother." So, Korean churches, keep sending out missionaries. But may God grant power and grace that Korean

---

[2] Related to me by Lindsay Brown of IFES.

missionaries would one day have the reputation of being the most humble servants in the world.

Kingdom Come in the Middle East

How about God's work in the Middle East?

A missionary traveled to Saudi Arabia, where she stayed with some Muslim friends. The lady of the house asked the missionary if she would come downstairs to see a new room she had decorated. Out of courtesy, she followed the lady downstairs where about eighty people had been waiting. The lady then asked the missionary to share with them about Isa (Jesus).

"But isn't that illegal in Saudi Arabia? Why do you want me to share with these people?"

The lady responded that they were all close family members or friends. And all were interested in the person of Jesus.

"How has this come about?" the missionary asked.

The lady replied, "You know that I have a Filipino housemaid. She sings all the time and looks so joyful. I asked her what she was singing about, and she explained she was singing songs of praise and thanksgiving to God for Jesus. I asked her to tell me more about him. Through her witness I became a Christian, then my husband; then we shared the gospel with these family members and friends. Some have come to faith; others are seeking. That's why I want you to share with them about Jesus and the Bible."[3] All this because of a Filipino maid singing praise to Jesus in a Muslim household in Saudi Arabia.

Kingdom Come in Africa

And from Africa to Africa, and Africa to the world.

A few weeks ago, I got an e-mail from a dear friend in Nigeria. I had asked him about his safety, as I knew that because of his outreach to Muslims he receives death threats two or three times each week. He replied to me, "As a matter of fact, last night I was

---

[3] Ibid.

told to come out of my house because Muslims were coming to attack me in the house where I live. But I stayed and prayed, and this is now morning and I am alive! Praise the Lord!"

I don't think my friend needs coffee to perk him up in the morning. "I'm alive! Praise the Lord!"—that will suffice.

In ten years their ministry has seen more than five thousand Islamic scholars turn to Christ. Seventy-eight have become missionaries. An Islamic court judge became a follower of Christ through this ministry. Through this judge alone, more than sixty Islamic clerics now worship Jesus. As we speak, however, the judge is recovering from injuries from being attacked by Muslim fundamentalists.

Just last month a few miles from my friend's house, a pastor and his six children were killed by Muslim fundamentalists. Pray for God's mercy in Nigeria!

But there is much work to be done toward the building of God's kingdom. According to the Joshua Project,[4] there are more than 6,500 unreached people groups in the world that represent more than 2.5 billion people. My mission field, Japan, is the largest unreached nation in the world.

Lord, may your kingdom come among the 6,500 unreached people groups in the world. Lord, mobilize your church toward that end. And for the building of God's kingdom—for the hallowing of God's name—we pray.

"YOUR WILL BE DONE"

"Your will be done" is the prayer for God's revealed will to be done, and an essential way that God's will is done and honored is when God's people obey—when we live out the purposes of God in our lives, when we live *for* God, in every aspect of our lives, with love for God with all our heart, soul, mind, and strength.

Hallowed be your name, your kingdom come, your will be done—worship, kingdom, and obedience. So, from the first three

---

[4] http://joshuaproject.net.

petitions we see that the purpose of life for every Christian from every nation is as follows.

1) Passionately pray for and pursue the global and eternal worship of and living for God.

Global and eternal worship starts on the individual level and also includes family and the church and culminates globally. As Christ's purpose for life is lived out by every Christian in every land, the gospel will flow naturally, powerfully, and passionately from every land to every land

Hallowed be your name! Your kingdom come! Your will be done! What is this but the passionate prayer and pursuit of global and eternal worship of and living for God?

Now let's move on to the second part of the Lord's Prayer, which has been described by some commentators as focusing on personal needs. But, as I alluded to before, I believe that these two sections in the Lord's Prayer are much more than just two sections with two different themes; rather, the two sections are very much related. Commentators, good commentators, suggest that the first three petitions focus on the preeminence of God while the final three focus on personal needs, but there is more than just that.

In the first half, Jesus teaches us to cry to God to accomplish through our prayers and lives God's purpose for global and eternal worship, and the second part is not just a prayer for personal needs, but it is a provision of all that is needed for such purpose of life as laid out in the first section.

2) Passionately pray for provision of all that is needed for such purpose of life as laid out in the first section.

Let me say this again: the second half of the Lord's Prayer is for provision of all that is needed for the purpose of life, which is to passionately pray for and pursue the global and eternal worship of and living for God (as expressed in the first half of the Lord's Prayer). The second half of the prayer is intimately related to the first half—not just that the first half is the big picture and the second is the little picture, or that the first half is the spiritual side and the second the earthly, or that the first half is corporate and the second half individual. The second half is prayer for the provision of all that is needed for the purposes expressed in the first half.

"GIVE US THIS DAY OUR DAILY BREAD"

The second half starts off, "Give us this day our daily bread"—a prayer for our basic needs. Toward the life that passionately prays for and pursues the global and eternal worship of and living for God, we have basic needs, such as bread. The standard is not luxury but sustenance.

We live in a country where we have to deliberately limit our food intake and the caloric content of our food. Has the prayer, "Give us this day our daily bread," become meaningless in our society and churches? And if not, then what could God be teaching you? Would you pray and ask the Lord about this? "Lord, why should I even pray this prayer? I don't *need to!*" "I have two cars. I have a retirement fund. I have disposable income." Why would the Lord have you pray, "Give us this day our daily bread"?

Only America could have invented such a term—*disposable income*. Essentially *disposable income* means that everything beyond daily bread, everything beyond sustenance, is one's own. Everything beyond daily bread is discretionary funds. Perhaps then the reason why Jesus teaches us to pray, "Give us this day our daily bread," is that we are to view every gift, every dollar, and every resource not as a personal slush fund but as provision to pursue passionately Christ's purpose for life—for the global and eternal worship of and living for God, and that our passionate living and generous giving toward such global purpose might even "foolishly" require us to tangibly need God's help for our daily bread.

"FORGIVE US OUR DEBTS AS WE HAVE FORGIVEN OUR DEBTORS"

Next comes the prayer for forgiveness and the power to forgive. This is a reminder of our most basic spiritual need—forgiveness. It's a reminder of our sinfulness and also of God's mercy. It's a reminder of the gospel, the very foundation of the purpose of God emphasized in the first half of the Lord's Prayer. The gospel is to be received and also extended to others.

Some of you perhaps know the story of the gospel in my life. One hundred years ago the gospel began to take root in Korea. The gospel reached my family through Presbyterian missionaries. It was faith that helped them endure one of the darkest periods of Korean history, the Japanese occupation from 1910 to 1945.

As many as thirty million Asians lost their lives at the hands of the Japanese Imperial Army. This was perhaps the greatest loss of human life in the history of mankind. My own great aunt was married off as a young teenager to avoid becoming one of the more than 150,000 Korean women and girls as young as twelve years old who were forced to be sex slaves of the Japanese army and endured rape dozens of times each day.

In the strange and beautiful providence of God, he saw fit to eventually send my father to America, only to have him later say good-bye to his son who was going back to Asia to bring the gospel to the land of his former enemy.

From every land to every land. Even from Korea to Japan. Glorious gospel design.

Forgiveness of the Japanese has been a complicated journey for me personally. Do you know how sometimes you can forgive someone for something, only to learn later much more about what actually happened? That was the situation for me. During my initial call to and service in Japan, I didn't even quite understand what it meant that for me, as a Korean, Japan was my enemy. It was actually during the years I was earning various graduate degrees and doing research that I learned more of the dark truths of that period of history.

But more than really just learning to forgive and love the Japanese over these years, I think what I've really learned the most about has been the gospel. I've learned about my own sinfulness and self-righteousness and about the stunning mercy that God would love someone like me.

So over the past nine years, it has been a privilege to serve God's gospel purposes in Japan, to live and serve alongside the Japanese, and to love and be loved by Japanese Christians. As I've said to many friends in the past, I'm the worst missionary in Japan. It's an evidence of God's grace that Japanese Christians would accept someone like me to serve among them. *Thank you, brothers and sisters in Japan.*

I lead a ministry called CBI Japan, which includes a graduate theological seminary called Christ Bible Seminary, church planting through All Nations Fellowship, and various outreaches in the city, including Heart and Soul and the soon-to-be-launched Heart and Soul Cafe.

About six years ago, the Lord gave us a vision to shine the light of Christ in the heart of the city of Nagoya. But with real estate infamously expensive, honestly there were times when I wondered why God would call us to pray for something that seemed almost impossible. During the real estate bubble (which burst in Japan about twenty years ago), a tiny 5-foot-by-7-foot slice of land in downtown Nagoya cost about $100,000.

Two years ago the Lord showed us an amazing property just three train stops away from Nagoya station (valued during the bubble at $8 million) with a sale price of $1.3 million. It was a huge bargain but still about $1.2 million more than I had ever raised.

We called for ninety days of prayer—and thanks to the many of you who prayed with us. Missionaries around the world donated $50,000, including missionaries serving in China, Latin

America, and Afghanistan. They emptied their two mites into the offering plate.

By day eighty-two God had provided $1.3 million. (Before you get too excited, let me add that a few years ago a Newark mosque had a special meeting to announce their hopes to buy a Methodist church building that had closed a few blocks down the road. It was up for sale for $1.5 million. They told their congregation that the purpose for buying it was to advance the kingdom of Allah. The next Friday they had $1.6 million.)

So the Lord provided for our new campus, but a few days later the property was seized by the courts after the business went bankrupt. And we were left wondering what in the world God was doing. John Piper said something, though, that has stuck in my mind and has been a great challenge to our team: "God cares more about how you react if you lose the property than about the property itself." So we continued to treasure God more than any treasure and to believe in the glory of God's plan (even though it seemed like plan B to us) and to wait upon him.

Then the Lord showed us an even more amazing property—2.5 times the land size, a larger building, and not three stops from Nagoya station with a five-minute walk.

We thought for sure it would cost at least $5 million to $6 million.

But I'm happy to share with you that this property officially became ours in March for $1.2 million.

We want to shine the light of Christ in the heart of the city where so many of the greatest social ills and hurting populations are. Studies show that as many as 9 percent of high school girls have participated in *enjo kosai*, a form of teenage prostitution. Even as many as 4 percent of middle school girls report having participated. With such practices and even the possession of child pornography being legal, Japan is not a safe place for young people. With bullying and some of the highest suicide rates in the world, Japan is not a safe place for young people.

So the Lord gave us a vision to establish in our new building the Heart and Soul Cafe, which will be a "safe space" ministry—a place where young people can be physically, relationally, emotionally, sexually, and spiritually safe, where they can find true safety in the gospel. We'd appreciate your prayers for our ministry and for the gospel to flourish in the largest unreached nation on earth, and we thank you for your prayers for Japan, especially since the earthquake, tsunami, and nuclear radiation crisis. We mourn the twenty thousand lives lost, most of whom didn't know Christ. But we believe that God is both sovereign over such tragedies and has gracious gospel purposes that will be revealed.

I believe that it is very likely that over the past two or three years more people have heard about and prayed for the Japanese people and the gospel work among the Japanese than at any other time in history. And I believe that so often God moves his people to pray prayers that he desires to answer.

So please pray for Japan.

"LEAD US NOT INTO TEMPTATION"

Temptation. This seems key. Between our individual salvation and the pursuit of global eternal worship of God lies temptation. What is this?

Perhaps for some, that temptation is the worshiping of, the hallowing of, God's very provision—daily bread, hoarded like the Israelites hoarding manna in the wilderness. Perhaps the temptation includes the idolizing of God's spiritual blessings as well, the idolizing of a kind of spiritual comfort.

This idolatry of Christian comfort is something that I can understand. It's the comfort of God's grace and love; the comfort of my own salvation; the comfort of a marvelous, guaranteed future. But rather than looking at our own blessed circumstances and then the unfortunate circumstances of others who are without Christ and saying, "Thank God I'm not them," we need to recognize that our circumstances are by the grace of God alone—and pray for mercy that we avoid the temptations of our blessed circumstances.

Have you in the West ever considered for a moment the absolute mercy and blessedness of being born into your circumstances? You could just as easily have been born in the slums of Bangladesh or as the son of a Shinto priest. Mercy and grace. If you had been born in the slums of Bangladesh or as the son of a Shinto priest, how would you want the Christians of North America to respond?

The temptation of spiritual hermitage.

The temptation of self-kingdom building.

The temptation of self-hallowing.

The temptation of *my* will be done.

These are the essences not of the Christian life but of hell.

As George MacDonald wrote, "The one principle of hell is 'I am my own.'"

In temptation there is not only the option of compromise but also the glory of "I choose you." In each episode of temptation, there is not merely the possibility of sin but also the opportunity to bring glory to God, as we say no to the temptation and yes to God—as we say, "Lord, in this temptation I choose you."

With every dollar, with every decision, with every opportunity, with every temptation—"Lord, I choose you!"

It's so easy for Christians to pray for and live for these verses in the second half of the prayer while skipping the first section that lays out the very purposes of God for our lives and God's purposes in his world. Too many Christians have made the second half, the provision of God, their purpose.

We live for material blessing.

We enjoy *our* salvation.

We pursue Christian living.

We desire protection from evil.

But these are not to be seen in isolation. They are all to be in support of, and in service toward, the fulfilling of the purposes of God revealed in the first section of the prayer.

It's like there's a war raging, but we are all staying far away from the battlefield where we've dug out our bunkers. We're hoarding all the food, provisions, tools, resources, and weapons, enjoying each other's company. We're putting up barbed wire and setting out sandbags and land mines on the perimeter while a war is being waged way out there. Those blankets, those food rations, those tools, those weapons, those soldiers, that barbed wire, and those sandbags were designed as provision for war. Those provisions are prayed for and are provided *to serve God's purposes* for this world and for our lives. They are for the global and eternal worship of and living for God. God provides those resources not as the purpose of life but toward the pursuit of his agenda.

"DELIVER US FROM EVIL"

There is severe and deadly persecution of the church in many nations around the world, especially in the 10/40 Window. The most severely persecuted church in the world is in North Korea. In North Korea, the greatest human challenges of the world are all combined: severe poverty, oppressive Communism, global isolation, no political freedom, no religious freedom, no gospel.

But the North Koreans, the Koreans who live in the north, are a wonderful, precious people. And they need our prayers.

In the amazing providence of God, just around the corner from our new building in downtown Nagoya is a North Korean elementary and secondary school. Just two weeks ago, I was able to meet the principal and take a tour of the school and greet many of the children.

From every nation *to* every nation. Even from Japan, even within Japan, to North Koreans.

Around North Korea, you can see signs with these words: "We have nothing to envy." Now, of course, this is ridiculous in a nation with so little food and no freedom or hope. But it wasn't always so. In the early 1900s the city of Pyong Yang was known as "the Jerusalem of the East." In 1907, the year of the Great Pyong Yang Revival, fifty thousand Koreans came to Christ.

But since 1995 more than four million North Koreans have

died of starvation. According to one source more than five hundred thousand have fled to China for survival,[5] mostly women, and 80 percent of them have been raped and sexually trafficked. As many as one million have been killed in concentration camps with cruel brutality.

Nowhere in the world is Christian persecution so fierce as in North Korea. Owning a Bible could get you killed or sent to a harsh labor camp. Despite the risks, the church is growing. There are an estimated four hundred thousand believers. North Korean Christians, who have nothing of worldly value, understand that, in Christ, they have nothing to envy.

But we Christians in America, we who seem to have everything—so much food, so much freedom, so many resources, and most of all, the gospel—we *envy*. We envy as we see the people around us and as we watch TV. We envy their house, their car, their position, their education, their looks, their family, their girlfriend, their boyfriend, and their spouse.

Christian, you have nothing to envy. You have everything. You have Jesus!

Can we not learn that important lesson that the North Korean government would teach us? We have nothing to envy.

WHERE TO FROM HERE?

So where do we go from here? Let me suggest a few things.

1) Revisit the gospel. Refocus on the gospel. Some have taught, about financial giving, to think about the gospel and then give in response to the gospel. It's the same for the whole of our lives. Rehearse the gospel, and live your life as an echo to the gospel.

Look at your life. Honestly, what does your life say about your purpose or goal in how you use your time, in how you spend money, in what drives you, in your passions, in what you pray about, and in how you view the world? Is your life a gospel-centered, gospel-focused, gospel-empowered, gospel-adoring, and gospel-advocat-

---

[5] http://Globaldayofprayer.com/uploads/1265272524_the_worst_human_rights_crisis_in_the_world _today.pdf.

ing life? To answer "I think so" is to answer no. So we need that gospel even more.

2) Repent. Let's not just talk casually and say, "Yeah, in this and that way my life is out of line with the purposes of God." May Christians not take any sin lightly. Our response to sin must not be resignation or "Oh, well," but, "Oh, Lord, have mercy! Change me. Turn me away from sin. Turn me toward yourself and your purposes."

3) Pray. Pray the Lord's Prayer. Pray the prayers of Scripture back to God. Pray God's purposes back to him. Make God's agenda your agenda and God's passions your passions.

Pray for the world. Hallowed be your name in Japan! Your kingdom come in North Africa! Your will be done in Vietnam! In the Lord's Prayer Jesus is teaching us and empowering us for prayer ministry for the world.

4) Finally, live it out. Live out the passions and purposes of God. How? Invest in God's purposes with the whole of your life.

It starts with the basic question, how are we to enjoy life properly? This is so basic but so easy to forget. Every gift of God is to be enjoyed as *from* God and not *like* it's a god. Everything that is enjoyed and captures our affection must be enjoyed theistically, and christocentrically. Every blessing must be recognized as a blessing from God and every resource mobilized toward his purposes.

Music is an example. I have a wonderful friend named David, who is the concertmaster of the Philadelphia Orchestra. He is an amazing musician. And he is a Christian. Now, music can be enjoyed atheistically or secularly or without reference to God. It can be received and enjoyed idolatrously—worshiped, in a sense, like a god. Or it can be employed *doxologically*, to the glory of God. It can be received and employed as a gift from God, for his glory, rather than worshiped like a god, stealing glory from the one, true God.

David gave an amazing performance during a benefit concert he did for our ministry back in 2003, and at the end, he had tears in his eyes—which brought tears to his wife, Jane's, eyes as well, as she said to my wife and me that she had never seen David cry before at a concert. I think that, in some sense, David understood the eternal purpose in his music at that benefit concert—what it means to enjoy and employ music doxologically, both for his personal doxology of God and also for the cause of global doxology.

The same can be said for law, business, sports, sales, and more.

If you are a doctor, enjoy and practice medicine doxologically, worshiping God with amazement for the healing power that he placed in the human body. Practice soberly, remembering that a healed or healthy sinner is still lost without Jesus. And practice medicine contextually, remembering the spiritually tragic global context of the unreached peoples of the world and finding ways to exercise the gifts and resources that God has given you to impact the eternal context of global gospel ministry.

I have seen God powerfully use medicine, music, architecture, sports, technology, and arts in missions.

Everyone reading this chapter has gifts that can be mobilized for global impact in missions. For example, do you speak English? God can use that. English teaching is the most common mission work in Japan.

So what I'm advocating is the stewardship of life with all things serving God's purposes and passions, and every gift and talent enjoyed and employed for God and his purposes. The easiest, clearest, most impacting, and at the same time the hardest way is with money.

THE HARDEST THING: MONEY

I know times are hard, and many are struggling. But in good times and bad Jesus's teaching remains the same: "Where your treasure is, there your heart will be also" (Matt. 6:21).

Money is often the best indicator of your heart passions and priorities—and thus perhaps the best place to start.

What is the value of $6,300?

I recently had the opportunity to meet a young teacher who

was in Cape Town as a volunteer for the Third Lausanne Congress on World Evangelization. He probably makes about $40,000 per year. What is the value of $6,300 for him? This young man told me he had previously been at a conference where I had challenged listeners to commit to investing 20 percent of their salaries in the future—10 percent for the church and 10 percent for missions. So he e-mailed me wanting to make a donation of $6,300 to bless global younger leaders at Lausanne III. What was the value of $6,300 for him and for the kingdom of God?

I was able to purchase laptops and iPods and flash drives filled with Christian resources and sermons and books. Fifteen flash drives went into places such as Serbia, India, China, Eastern Europe, and the Middle East. iPods with audio recording and video capabilities went into Latin America, one to Eastern Europe, another to Nigeria, and another to Egypt. One laptop went into China, another to Eastern Europe, and another to an African leader who had been praying for a laptop. Five hundred dollars went into Africa, $500 into Mongolia, $500 into Latin America, $500 into the Middle East and North Africa, and $500 into Eastern Europe.

The value of money is amazing when it is invested in God's kingdom. The returns are eternal. What is the value of $6,300? It is priceless. It is stunning how God can use even the simplest of giving such as that of a young man with a small salary determining to give just 10 percent of it for global missions.

What of the resources that God has given you could be used for such glorious global eternal impact? Even if you are just a young teacher with a modest salary, you can make significant global, eternal impact.

Imagine what God could do if you would invest just a portion of what he has given to you for his purposes, for his kingdom, and for his glory. If you make $25,000 per year, you are among the richest 10 percent of the world. You are über-rich. In fact, if you make $2,500 per year, you are among the richest 15 percent of the world. And if you make $50,000 per year, you are among the richest 1 percent of the world.

One of the seminars at a conference I was at recently was titled, "How to Become a Billionaire." Unfortunately, I was giving a seminar at the same time, so I couldn't go. So, I'm sorry, I have no good tips for you. But I do want to talk about how you can become a millionaire.

There are many sites online with "millionaire calculators." You can figure out how long it will be until you become a millionaire, depending on how much you have and how much you save and assuming some percentage return on your savings such as 7 or 8 percent. So, if right now you have no money at all, but you're determined to become a millionaire, let me try to help you out. This is illuminating.

If you set aside only $5,000 per year, at 8 percent return, you'll become a millionaire in thirty-six years and ten months. The point: the target is in sight! It's doable.

Or let's say you invest $5,000 per year in global kingdom building. In thirty-six years and ten months, you will have been able to invest the equivalent of about $1 million in Jesus's name-hallowing, kingdom-building, eternity-altering, global mission work. *The point: the target is in sight! It's doable.*

I guarantee you that in heaven the return on all the funds invested in God's kingdom will yield you *much more* than 8 percent. What wonderful discipleship to be able to tell your kids and your grandkids that you invested $1 million in global missions!

As a general guideline on giving, if you want my opinion, you could consider for a salary of up to $50,000 an appropriate giving budget of 10 percent for the church and 5 percent for global missions. Even at this salary level, you should be able to get to the $1 million mark if you start early.

For salaries of $50,000 to $150,000, give 10 percent to the church and 10 percent to global missions.

For salaries of $150,000 to $500,000, give 10 percent or more to the church and 20 percent to global missions.

For salaries of $500,000 and upwards, give 10 percent or more to the church and 40 percent or more to global missions.

This world will be transformed if God gives you all the grace and the guts to do this.

INVEST WISELY

A month ago I was pretty excited because I heard about a potential $1 million gift to our ministry. We were, and still are, about $100,000 short for paying for the earthquake reinforcement beams that we had to put on our new building. So a $1 million gift would have made a huge impact on our ministry.

But then I heard that the businessman decided to give the $1 million to the Red Cross instead. Now, I have nothing against the Red Cross. I've donated blood to the Red Cross a few times. But I didn't donate my blood to the Red Cross instead of, for example, Dave Sitton's ministry To Every Tribe. I don't think Dave wants you to send your blood donation—at least not that kind of blood donation.

Please, please, invest wisely and eternally—certainly in Christian ministries, and especially for global mission. Please! That $1 million donation to the Red Cross will go toward paying for a yearly advertising/promotions budget of $130 million.

So please make investments that will make eternal impact, and find missions organizations and missionaries where your $6,300, your 10 percent, or your $1 million is going to make the greatest kingdom impact, the greatest name-hallowing impact. There are so many really worthy, small, struggling missions groups that are praying for donors like you.

GIVING AS A FAMILY

Perhaps some reading this chapter would, by faith, like to commit to trying such giving today. I know you will not regret it. If you want to commit your efforts to some level of this type of giving—whether a certain percentage or *everything* beyond a certain amount—would you right now, in the quietness of your own heart, let God know?

I want to encourage you to make these kinds of decisions as a family. There is generally reluctance among parents to discuss finances with their children. They want them neither to share in the burdens nor to get spoiled by the abundances. But transparency in finances with your children allows for amazing opportunity for their discipleship. It's clear from Jesus's emphasis on teaching about money and the content of that teaching that it's one of the most telling factors about your faith and priorities, and, if so, it will be one of the most important lessons you can teach your children.

A few years ago my daughter asked me, "Papa, are we poor?" That was when I realized, "We need to talk more openly with our kids about finances and biblical stewardship." I mean, what do you say to such a question from your daughter?

So my wife, Pearl, and I decided to talk about our finances as a family every Thanksgiving, to budget together our church and missions giving, and to decide together as a family how to invest those God-given resources. We tell the kids, "This is how much money God has provided for our family each month, this is how much we spend on various things, and this is how much we would like to set aside for global missions." And then we talk about different missionaries and mission groups that each of our kids would like to support.

It's not a huge amount, but it's a percentage along the lines that I encouraged you to consider. It will eventually allow our family the privilege and joy to be able to invest for God's global glory the equivalent of more than $1 million. If God could do that through a missionary family of seven, what could he do through your family?

The basic principle is that with the more you earn, you have increased ability to invest in God's kingdom building, not merely in absolute dollar amounts but in increased percentage of your giving. As Randy Alcorn says, "God prospers me not to raise my standard of living, but to raise my standard of giving."[6]

NOT AFRAID TO BLEED

For the Great Commission, and for the accomplishing of the Lord's purpose in life, great sacrifices are needed. We need sacrifice by those who will go, laying aside comfort, family, and the American dream. And we need sacrifice by those who will send.

A Pakistani Christian was riding in a New York City taxi driven by a Pakistani Muslim and asked curiously, "How is kingdom umma going?" "Great," the taxi driver replied. "Americans are so afraid of us. They are so afraid to bleed." No doubt there are many Christians in America who are afraid to bleed, afraid of sacrifice, and afraid to lose their comforts. But I also do believe that there are American Christians and Christians around the world who are not afraid to bleed and sacrifice for Jesus.

KILLED FOR NORTH KOREA

In South Africa at the 2010 Third Lausanne Congress,[7] a high school girl from North Korea shared her story. She was born into a wealthy family, her father an assistant to the North Korean leader Kim Jong Il. Eventually her father's political fortunes shifted, and after being politically persecuted by the North Korean government, he, his wife, and his daughter escaped to China.

In China, a relative brought them to church where her parents came to know Christ. A few months later, however, her pregnant mother died from leukemia. Her father started to study the Bible with missionaries, and eventually the Lord gave him a strong desire to become a missionary to North Korea. But in 2001 he was reported as a Christian, arrested by the Chinese police, and returned to North Korea. Forced to leave his daughter behind in China, he spent three years in prison.

---

[6] Randy Alcorn, *The Treasure Principle: Discovering the Secret of Joyful Giving* (Sisters, OR: Multnomah, 2001).
[7] See http://www.lausanne.org/en/gatherings/cape-town-2010.html.

Eventually he was able to return to China where he was briefly reunited with his daughter. Soon after, however, he gathered Bibles, having resolved to return to North Korea to share Christ among that hopeless people. In 2006 he was discovered by the North Korean government and arrested. There has since been no word from him. In all probability, he has been shot to death publicly for treason.

INVESTING OUR EVERYTHING

There are those around the world who have risked or given their very lives for the purpose of God—for the hallowing of God's name. Some of you reading this chapter may be feeling a distinct, undeniable passion to go into the world as a missionary—the cry of your heart, the conviction of your life, is to invest your everything for God's global glory. Your heart prays, "Lord, hallowed be your name among the unreached of the world," and your heart conviction compels you to go and invest your life to see that hallowing happen.

If so, I invite you to talk with your family, your friends, and the leadership of the church. Ask for their prayers and counsel. And pursue God's calling with prayer and passion. You will not regret it.

UNLESS SOMEONE STOPS YOU

My advice? Unless someone biblically stops you, go. Unless or until your mission board or your church leaders stop you and tell you that you're not fit for missionary service, I don't believe that you would be doing wrong to pursue missions overseas or to pursue simply being a Christian among an unreached people as a tentmaker.

If God stops you, accept it humbly, and try to be the best sender your church has ever known. But if you go, I urge you to consider the unreached, to consider the hardest of mission fields (such as the Muslims or the Japanese) and to go while you are young. Expect things to be hard. Expect opposition. But persevere.

We have friends ministering among the precious Hyugur people in China; apparently on average it takes about forty exposures to the gospel before a Hyugur Muslim believes. Forty!

As you share the gospel with those near and far, with family members and strangers, persevere. How many could be won to Christ if we would persevere through forty gospel sharings?

THE GLOBAL FLOW OF THE GOSPEL

In 2007 the North Korean girl, who at the time was not a Christian, was given the opportunity to go to South Korea. While still in China waiting at the Korean consulate in Beijing to go to South Korea, she saw Jesus in a dream. Jesus, with tears in his eyes, called her by name and said, *How much longer are you going to keep me waiting? Walk with me. Yes, you lost your earthly father, but my Father is your heavenly Father and whatever has happened to you is because I love you.*

She knelt and prayed to God for the first time and realized, "God my Father loves and cares for me so very much that he sent his Son Jesus to die for me." She prayed, "God, here I am. I lay down everything and give you my heart, my soul, my mind, and my strength. Please use me as you will."

Now God has given her a great love for North Korea. She shares, "Just as my father was used there for God's kingdom, I now desire to be obedient to God. I want to bring the love of Jesus to North Korea."

What a fool! If you escape hell on earth, you don't go back. What a fool for Christ. But this is the path and global flow of the gospel—from everywhere to everywhere—even North Korea, even hell on earth.

How many of us so easily choose the path of comfort and safety—the path that is our answer to the question, what is best for me? We seek the provisions of God but neglect his purposes. And in holding on to those provisions, we halt the advance of his kingdom, which Jesus teaches us to pray for and to pursue.

So many of those whom God has used to make some of the

greatest kingdom impact have not made decisions based on "What is best for me?" or "My will be done." Rather, they made decisions based on an undeniable, unshakable, "illogical," "foolish" passion for Jesus Christ and for the building of his global kingdom.

For this girl's father, there was a "safe" path before him. The door was open for him to go to South Korea, where there was political and religious freedom, where his family could have been safe, where there was daily bread and much, much more.

He could have come to the United States and pursued the American dream and enjoyed worshiping God at a great church, freedom, and a weeknight Bible study. No prison, no persecution, no pain. Instead, he chose the path of danger that led him, Bibles in hand, back to North Korea.

Now his daughter has determined to follow that same path— both father and daughter, passionately praying for and pursuing the worship of God among the North Koreans so that the global gospel flow might not end simply with them lifting their hands in a comfortable pew in a comfortable place enjoying the gospel while North Koreans go to hell without Christ.

Hallowed be your name, O Lord, in North Korea!

Hallowed be your name, O Lord, in all the earth!

May God grant us the grace to serve with undeniable, unshakable, illogical, and foolish passion for the hallowing of God's name and the building of his global kingdom.

5

TO OUR NEIGHBORS AND THE NATIONS

Ed Stetzer

Modern Christians, particularly of the Western world, seem to trend toward one of two paths when they talk about God's mission. Either they will set off down a "sent-ness" path by emphasizing the church as being *sent* and what it means to be *missional*, or they will go down a "nations" path by emphasizing the church as the one *sending* around the world. While these two paths are not incompatible, they seem too often to be followed in divergent directions. The reason for this is that they often focus on different parts of the *missio Dei* (mission of God). Yet, I think by exploring the commissions of Jesus, we get a better picture of God's mission—we understand more clearly our missiology.

In the past century, there has been a tremendous amount written on missiology. But as I write on missiology in this chapter, I do so because I believe there is still more that needs to be said, and this conversation is necessary for the health and growth of the church. I would take another step and suggest that the church today desperately needs to remain engaged in this conversation. A proper theological diet needs a healthy portion of missiology, and perhaps the best way to do so is by examining the commissions of Jesus.

In this chapter, I will focus on all four of the commissions of Jesus. We will examine what it means to be a missional, missions-minded, gospel-centered, Spirit-empowered church from the four commissions of Jesus, so that his name and his fame would be more widely known.

WE ARE SENT: A SENDING FOCUS

The church is a *sent* people, and the sending focus of God's people is captured in the Gospel of John. In John 20, after the resurrection, Jesus appears in the flesh to his disciples. In the first commission of Jesus, beginning in verse 19, John writes:

> In the evening of that first day of the week, the disciples were gathered together with the doors locked because of their fear of the Jews. Then Jesus came, stood among them, and said to them, "Peace to you!" Having said this, He showed them His hands and His side. So the disciples rejoiced when they saw the Lord.[1]

And he says to them again in verse 21 (note the key phrase in italics):

> Jesus said to them again, "Peace to you! *As the Father has sent Me, I also send you.*"

Jesus is both the sent and the sender. Readers are forced to make a hermeneutical decision. Is Jesus's command to his disciples also applicable to us? Certainly, when you look at the commissions of Jesus, there have been times in the history of the church when Christians have said, "No, that just applies to those who heard the voice of Jesus in the first century." But hopefully we will move beyond this limited application of Scripture and recognize that when Jesus speaks to his disciples here, at this moment, his command also applies to us. Jesus is both the sent one, and the sender of his people. Consequently, the church, as the body of Christ, is both a sent people and a sending people.

Defining Mission

We are sent on mission. But what does that mean? Am I now a missionary? Am I missional? And here's where our language requires clarification.

---

[1] All Scripture quotations in this chapter are taken from the Holman Christian Standard (HCSB) version of the Bible.

Defining mission might seem at first to be a relatively simple task. But, as you start, you see that there are challenges in defining the term *mission*. In 2010 David Hesselgrave and I edited a book on missiology called *MissionShift*.[2] The first third of the book is dedicated to defining and describing the terms *mission, missions, missional, missio Dei*, and *missionary*. Charles Van Engen, Keith Eitel, Enoch Wan, Darrell L. Guder, Andreas Köstenberger, and I interact and respond to one another regarding how we define and/or describe mission. It was a fascinating conversation. In my chapter I conclude, "We need . . . a 'cohesive, consistent, focused, theologically deep, missiologically broad, contextually appropriate, and praxeologically effective, evangelical missiology.'"[3] Indeed, we need a clear understanding of mission.

The word *mission* comes from a Latin word meaning "to send." That does not necessarily help us fully define what mission is biblically. Being sent and sending are major themes in the story of Scripture, but limiting our definition to the sending actions of God limits our view of mission in some significant ways. First, sending alone does not entail other important, mission-centered themes in the biblical stories. Second, broadening how we speak of mission also helps us to locate our actions in God's grand plan for history, so this allows us to acknowledge that sending is always for a purpose. Avery Willis, an author and missiologist (recently deceased), describes mission in such eschatological terms. Willis says:

> By mission I mean the total redemptive purpose of God to establish his kingdom. Missions, on the other hand, [as contrasted with mission] is the activity of God's people the church to proclaim and to demonstrate the kingdom of God in the world.[4]

Willis goes on to clarify the difference between mission and

---

[2] David J. Hesselgrave and Ed Stetzer, eds., *MissionShift: Global Mission Issues in the Third Millennium* (Nashville: Broadman, 2010).
[3] Ibid., 80.
[4] Avery Willis, "Biblical Basis for Mission," available on International Mission Board website (1979, repr. 1992), http:www.imb.org/core/biblicalbasis/introduction.htm, accessed on December 16, 2011.

missionaries, saying, "Missionaries are set apart by God and the church to cross natural and cultural barriers with the gospel."[5] Mission, therefore, is conceived as the total redemptive purpose of God to establish his kingdom, and missionaries are those agents who carry out God's redemptive purposes through the church in a variety of contexts.

It is important to note here that God *has a mission* and *is on a mission*. We find this in the biblical story. God is both sender and sent in Christ. God, the Father, is the source of mission. He sent his Son, who embodies God's mission and accomplishes it. God's mission is then extended and applied through the ministry of the Spirit, for it is the Spirit who calls, equips, and empowers the people of God. The mission is therefore God's. He sends to accomplish his mission—the redemption of his whole creation. Jesus consistently spoke of himself as being "sent" in John's Gospel and subsequently commissioned his disciples for this same purpose (John 17:3, 8, 18, 21, 23, 25). As the "sent" people of God, the church is the instrument of his mission (John 20:21). Missions flows from the mission of God.

Defining Missionary

So, what's a missionary? Some of you reading this are missionaries (according to Willis's definition). You cross cultural barriers in Jesus's name so his fame would be more widely known. In some sense, however, as Charles Spurgeon said, "Every Christian is either a missionary or an imposter."[6] So, how should we use the term *missionary?*

Let me suggest first an answer that not everyone will agree with. Precision in language is not as important as the emphasis on being sent. So, it is at this point that I like what Spurgeon says. Here, it seems to me that everyone should be able to agree with what he meant. When Spurgeon said, "Every Christian is

---

[5] Ibid.
[6] Charles H. Spurgeon, "A Sermon and a Reminiscence," *Sword and the Trowel* (March 1873), http://www.spurgeon.org/s_and_t/srmn1873.htm.

either a missionary or an impostor," he was saying that we all are sent by Jesus and are called to live in light of that sending. Christians are called to live on mission.

Second, I prefer to use "missionary" to refer to particular people who pursue a particular calling. While some might say, however, "All Christians are missionaries," I would not typically phrase it that way. I would emphasize the sent-ness of all Christians to live on mission. Missionaries are those with particular ministry and calling to cross cultural barriers to make disciples of Jesus. We live in a pluralistic world today. People once had to cross regional and geographical borders to do the work of missions. Now, many of us can engage readily in cross-cultural conversations without leaving our own cities. These opportunities will continue to grow.

Even as I more narrowly define *missionary*, I still think that the first step is to confirm the sent-ness of all disciples.

Defining Missional

I (and others) use the term *missional* to describe a mission-shaped life. *Missional* is simply the adjectival use of the word *mission*. In other words, if I'm living a missional life, I'm living a life shaped by God's mission, which is again simply a Latin-based word centered on the concept of being sent. As we have seen, the root of the word does not give a full picture of living missionally, for sent-ness implies purpose.

John 20:21 is ultimately about God's sending and about the fact that we are sent. So to be faithful to this text, we focus on mission as sent-ness. Jesus said if you're a follower of Christ, if you've been born again by the power of the gospel, you are sent. It doesn't matter what you call it. What matters is that when you've encountered God, when you've been made new in Christ, that you stand before God, saying "Here I am, Lord. Send me."

"I thought only missionaries were sent?" you ask. Well, they are. Those who live missionally are sent, too. "Well, missionaries seem more sent than us. I mean, they get odd clothes. They live in tents. They eat bugs. They are different."

And after knowing and encouraging vocational missionaries for decades, I can say with certitude that, yes, missionaries are different. But missionaries are not aliens. Their spiritual responsibility for the mission of God is the same as those who live in their hometown for their entire lives. The difference between the missionary and County Seat First Church member lies not in their sent-ness but in their context and the ways that they pursue their life of mission.

"As the Father has sent Me, I also send you." God is gracious. He is good. He is merciful. He is holy. God is also a sender. We forget this. God demonstrates it in the Old Testament when he sends Abraham to be blessed and to be a blessing to others. Jonah is sent. God asks the prophet Isaiah, "Who should I send? Who will go for Us?" Isaiah replied, "Here I am. Send me" (Isa. 6:8).

We could go on and on and on with examples of God's sending—from Genesis to Malachi. God sends because he is a sender. And, of course, God demonstrates his sending nature in the New Testament. As we have seen in John 20:21, Jesus says, "As the Father has sent Me, I also send you." The Father, in his sent-ness, has eternally begotten (whatever that means in Trinitarian terms!) the same nature in Jesus. Jesus, therefore, also has a nature of sent-ness. As Jesus's disciples become transformed into the image of Christ, they, in turn, put on his sent-ness.

Sent-ness

We do not want to miss the scriptural theme of sent-ness, because it defines so much of who God is, what he is doing, and who we are. For example:

The Father sent the Son. In John 20:21 Jesus says, "As the Father has sent Me, I also send you."

The Father sent the Spirit (in Jesus's name). In John 14:26, Jesus says, "But the Counselor, the Holy Spirit—the Father will send

Him in My name—will teach you all things and remind you of everything I have told you." So the Father sent the Son, and the Father sends the Spirit in Jesus's name.

Jesus is sent to establish his kingdom. The movement of being sent continues. The Son comes and establishes his kingdom. In Mark 1:15 Jesus says, "The time is fulfilled, and the kingdom of God has come near. Repent and believe in the good news!" Jesus is not speaking chronologically, describing the time in space when the kingdom will be ultimately established. Jesus is speaking geographically, describing the location of the kingdom. It is as if Jesus is saying, "Here it is!" The kingdom has come because the Son has come. The sending of the Trinity gives birth to a movement among his people.

The church is sent in the kingdom's wake (the sent-ness of the bride), continuing the trajectory of the recurring theme of this sent-ness. The church is birthed out of a movement (kingdom) of people empowered by the Spirit.

The Son builds the church by placing people in his kingdom. Jesus is building his church. He said he would build his church in Matthew 16, but in Colossians he tells us how. In Colossians 1:13 the Spirit testifies, "He has rescued us from the domain of darkness and transferred us into the kingdom of the Son He loves." God is rescuing us, his people. Why? Because God is sending the church as agents of God's kingdom in the world.

The Spirit empowers the church. The Spirit empowers the church to imitate God's sent-ness. As the Son builds the church by placing people in the kingdom, the Spirit empowers the church to live as the sent agents of the kingdom of God. Second Corinthians 5:20 says, "Therefore, we are ambassadors for Christ, certain that God is appealing through us. We plead on Christ's behalf, 'Be reconciled to God.'" The church is a network of ambassadors for Christ.

Ambassadors

In Ephesians 6:20 Paul says, "For this I am an ambassador in chains." Paul says in 2 Corinthians 5:20, "Therefore, we are ambassadors for Christ, certain that God is appealing through us. We plead on Christ's behalf, 'Be reconciled to God.'"

The church is an outpost of light in the darkness. In the military, an outpost is a group of soldiers stationed away from the main force. The outpost isn't the main force, but it represents the main force. As an outpost, the church isn't the main force, but it represents the main force. The church is in the world like an embassy is in the country in which its ambassador is stationed. The church is an initial point of contact for the kingdom of God, as God's people are interspersed amidst humanity. We do not plead with others from long distance; we plead with them up close and personally. We are sent people, meeting others in their home countries. We must build relationships with them, both inside and outside the embassy. We are not sent in power. We are sent to serve and build relationships with others to share the truths of the gospel with them. This is the nature of God's kingdom. As Jesus forms a community of the kingdom with the good news of the kingdom, the people he has purchased with his own blood (Acts 20:28; Titus 2:14) unify to accomplish God's purposes.

I grew up on Long Island outside of New York City. We knew ambassadors. They were the people with the cool cars that had flags and didn't pay parking tickets. But in Paul's day, ambassadors had a different social status than what I encountered in New York. Ambassadors today are high-ranking diplomatic officials. They are an indication that one political power sought a good working relationship with a second one. Ambassadors are sent for the purpose of establishing friendship, goodwill, and relationships for working together.

Yet, in the days of the New Testament, Rome did not send out ambassadors. They did not have to. Rome sent out conquering armies with governors who ruled over the conquered nation. That's how Rome established its authority with neighboring nations. But Rome would receive ambassadors, from as far away as India, and the Roman emperor bragged that ambassadors would come to Rome and entreat the emperor to have mercy. They'd say, "Please don't conquer us. Don't send one of those conquering armies and a ruling governor, but instead let us be an ally, a vassal state on the border, on the edge of the empire. Let us live." Rather than sending out ambassadors, the Roman Empire sent out armies and then governors to rule the conquered. Nations near the edges of the empire would send ambassadors to negotiate for peace or perhaps for status as a vassal state. The strong did not send out ambassadors. The weak did.

The all-powerful Roman Empire wouldn't send out ambassadors to those that didn't matter; but the all-powerful, loving, good, sovereign, perfect, and merciful God says that we're ambassadors for Christ, the king of a far greater kingdom. So this glorious, all-powerful God sends ambassadors on his behalf. It is a glorious scandal that confounds the wisdom of this world.

Clarifying Missional

Francis DuBose was the first person to write a book using the term *missional* the way many use it today. In his book *God Who Sends*, DuBose simply walks through the Scriptures, identifying places where God demonstrates his sent-ness.[7] As you begin to examine the Scriptures, understanding the heart and the mission of God, you begin to see with fresh eyes that we are a people made new in Christ to live as agents of his mission. This shapes us. This causes us to live sent. That's what missional is. If you're a missionary to the Pokot in Africa, you're sent. If you're living as a Christian in Pittsburgh, you're sent. We're all sent. The question is, where and among whom?

Michael Oh expresses it well when he describes the mission as "from everywhere to everywhere." The reality is that all of God's people are redeemed by the power of Christ, made new in relationship with him, and are now called to live sent. All of the talk about God's greatness, if we fail to understand that his greatness is intended to compel us toward mission, is descriptive

---

[7] Francis M. DuBose, *God Who Sends: A Fresh Quest for Biblical Mission* (Nashville: Broadman Press, 1978).

but morally vacuous. "As the Father has sent Me," Jesus said, "I also send you."

For some of you, this terminology will be new. Don't spend too much time worrying about using trendy words. As I wrote in *MissionShift*, "The making of definitions is in the nature of thinking. The describing of effective actions is in the nature of doing." The reality is that when all is said and done, too much will have been said and not enough will have been done. So, don't trip over the terms. Rather, spend time living intentionally. Marvel that you've encountered a good, perfect, holy, loving, and merciful God, and are in turn accountable to Jesus's command, "As the Father has sent Me, I also send you."

You're not all that God has called you to be, as a follower of Jesus, if you're missions-minded but not engaged in God's mission here and now. One of the temptations might be that you leave this information on your desk and say, "What we need to do is to give more and to go more." I know a lot of churches that are very missions-minded but are not particularly missional. In other words, they want to pay somebody else and outsource the mission of God. You should give and go more. We all should. But we also need to live as those who are sent here and now. At the end of the day, every believer has to listen to the words of Jesus, "As the Father has sent me, so send I you." The only rightful, appropriate response is, "Here I am, Lord; send me."

WE'RE SENT TO ALL PEOPLES: A NATIONS FOCUS

Scripture declares that you and I are sent to all peoples. In Matthew 28:18–20, the second commission of Jesus (often called the *Great* Commission), Jesus says:

> All authority has been given to Me in heaven and on earth. Go, therefore, and make disciples of all nations, baptizing them in the name of the Father and of the Son and of the Holy Spirit, teaching them to observe everything I have commanded you. And remember, I am with you always, to the end of the age.

The meaning of the phrase "to all nations," or *panta ta ethne* in the original (Greek) language, is debated. Many missiologists want to interpret the meaning as ethno-linguistic people groups. Others want to interpret the meaning as *ethno-nationalism.*

Based on even the most limited reading of the text, Jesus meant—at the very least—the Gentiles. But the disciples living during this moment in redemptive history understood much more than that. Volumes of books have been written on the meaning of the Great Commission, but if John 20:21 points to living sent, we need to explore why so many see the Great Commission as something we can finish by going to every tribe.

Jesus says, "On this rock I will build My church" (Matt. 16:18). Jesus announces "I will build my church," and the disciples, in response, went out and planted churches. So why do so many of Jesus's disciples travel so far? Paul says, "I have strongly desired for many years to come to you whenever I travel to Spain." Andrew went north into parts of Europe. Bartholomew made it as far as the Caspian Sea (according to legend). Thomas probably made it as far as India. Jesus's disciples traveled all around the world. Why? When they heard the words of Jesus, what caused them to think of this *panta ta ethne* ("all the nations") that moved them to go so far and preach to so many?

Christians trend toward two paths. One path is the path of sent-ness, the missional path. The other is the path of the nations, the missions path. But we don't need merely one or the other. We need both.

The context and the timing of the Great Commission in God's redemptive plan and mission explicitly pointed the disciples to something much greater than in the past. It was a pivotal moment. Jesus actually reversed the mission in a sense—he changed its direction. In the Old Testament, Israel was called to live in such a way that the nations would come to Jerusalem. In the New Testament, we find Jesus sending his disciples to the nations for God's glory. In Revelation 7:9–10 we see where the movement ends:

> After this I looked, and there was a vast multitude from every nation, tribe, people, and language, which no one could number, standing before the throne and before the Lamb. They were robed in white with palm branches in their hands. And they cried out in a loud voice: "Salvation belongs to our God, who is seated on the throne, and to the Lamb!"

This passage of Scripture reminds us that the throne room is surrounded by men and women from every tongue, tribe, and nation. Here they are giving praise to the Lamb. I would point out that there appears to be an ethno-linguistic thread through the Scripture. Every tongue, tribe, and nation is a thread woven through Scripture from the beginning all the way to the end.

A God Who Scatters

If we go all the way back to the beginning, we can see this ethno-linguistic thread. It begins in Genesis 11 with God scattering humankind. At the Tower of Babel, God is making nations. God has a redemptive plan. Genesis 11:1–9 says:

> At one time the whole earth had the same language and vocabulary. As people migrated from the east, they found a valley in the land of Shinar and settled there. They said to each other, "Come, let us make oven-fired bricks." They used brick for stone and asphalt for mortar. And they said, "Come, let us build ourselves a city and a tower with its top in the sky. Let us make a name for ourselves; otherwise, we will be scattered over the face of the whole earth." Then the LORD came down to look over the city and the tower that the men were building. The LORD said, "If they have begun to do this as one people all having the same language, then nothing they plan to do will be impossible for them. Come, let Us go down there and confuse their language so that they will not understand one another's speech." So from there the LORD scattered them over the face of the whole earth, and they stopped building the city. Therefore its name is called Babylon, for there the LORD confused the language of the whole earth, and from there the LORD scattered them over the face of the whole earth.

God scatters and makes the nations for a specific purpose. He scatters them, and then he chooses a people for himself.

God scatters to reunite. God sends Israel to bring the scattered nations *up to* Jerusalem. This idea that mission never existed in the Old Testament is a missiological error. God sent the people of Israel on a mission. We forget the mission of God in the Old Testament, and sometimes we think the only time we see God calling his people to reach the unreached is in Matthew 28. The Great Commission is not the first time that God calls his people to go to the nations.

God sends Israel to bring the nations *up* to Jerusalem. Jerusalem was a city on a hill. Anyone traveling to the capital city would have to walk up to the city, literally. The distinction between the Old and New Testaments in regard to the mission of God is the role of God's agents at different points in redemptive history. All of God's ambassadors serve the same overall mission (the *missio Dei*), but not all serve in the same role. Israel's role, recorded in the Old Testament, was to lead the nations up to Jerusalem to worship the one true God.

When the disciples heard "go to the nations," they were living in a time when the Old Testament was recent history. The Bible for first-century Christians was Genesis through Malachi. In Psalm 57:9 the psalmist writes, "I will praise You, Lord, among the peoples. I will sing praises to You among the nations." That was Israel's role. "For your faithful love is as high as the heavens. Your faithfulness reaches to the clouds. God, be exalted above the heavens; let Your glory be over the whole earth" (vv. 10–11). In Isaiah 2:3 (a wonderful key passage highlighting the mission of God in the Old Testament), Isaiah prophesies, "And many peoples will come and say, 'Come, let us go up to the mountain of the LORD, to the house of the God of Jacob. He will teach us about His ways so that we may walk in His paths.' For instruction will go out of Zion and the word of the LORD from Jerusalem." Verse 2 says, "All nations will stream to it."

That was the plan. But the plan was not fully accomplished.

The nations were not praising God in Jerusalem with many tongues. Yet, God was not done—he just turned the mission in a new direction.

God's Sovereign Sign and Plan

God, through his Holy Spirit, brought all tongues, tribes, and nations to Jerusalem to inaugurate his mission. In Acts 2 Luke writes, "When the day of Pentecost had arrived, they were all together in one place. Suddenly a sound like that of a violent rushing wind came from heaven, and it filled the whole house where they were staying. And tongues, like flames of fire that were divided, appeared to them and rested on each one of them" (vv. 1–4). The prophecies of old were realized through the power of the Spirit at Pentecost.

Christians interpret Luke's account of Pentecost differently, particularly as it relates to the gift of tongues. But there are some tongues we all agree on, because at this point in Scripture, speaking in tongues served as an undeniable sign. They were all filled with the Holy Spirit, and they began to speak in different languages as the Spirit gave each the ability. So, all around, people were hearing in their own language.

Pentecost is not simply an outpouring of the Holy Spirit. It is that, and so much more. Pentecost is a sign that redirects God's mission. The mission of God went *out from* Jerusalem, not through political might or warring nations but through the gospel proclamation of faithful churches as a tool for his subversive kingdom.

God has a sovereign sign, and he also has a sovereign plan. In Acts 2 God gives his people a sign, but in Acts 1 he also gives them his plan. Luke writes, "You will receive power when the Holy Spirit has come on you, and you will be My witnesses in Jerusalem, in all Judea and Samaria, and to the ends of the earth" (v. 8). Jesus redirects the mission: before, the uttermost parts of the earth had to come to Jerusalem; now, Jesus says, you'll go *from* Jerusalem to Judea, to Samaria, and to the uttermost parts.

Every Nation

God will be praised by women and men from every nation. We saw it in Revelation 7. God scattered from the idolatrous situation surrounding the Tower of Babel and made nations. God sends Israel to bring the nations up to Jerusalem. He has a sign and a plan for them when they get there.

So why is the Great Commission great? Jesus says, "Go, therefore, and make disciples of all nations." So at this moment the mission shifts in Jesus's words from a centripetal mission—*up to* Jerusalem—to a centrifugal mission   go therefore *out from* this place. Jesus tells us later that we'll go out from Jerusalem to Judea to Samaria to the ends of the earth. Because of his death and resurrection he moves the mission in a new direction: victory over death, sin, the grave, and hell.

In the summer of 2011 I traveled to Turkey. While there, I was burdened to see a fledgling church with so few workers. It's a slow work in Turkey, and there are challenges to working in a predominately Muslim context. I couldn't help but grieve over seeing the church struggle. You and I can't "not grieve" when we understand the context and the text of the Great Commission.

There are seventy million Turks and just a few thousand believers in Turkey. Yet this is where we find the seven churches in the book of Revelation. This is where the first seven ecumenical councils of the church were held. This place, this formerly thriving center of Christianity, now has only a few thousand people who would claim the name of Jesus Christ.

Christians need a heart for the nations because God has a heart for the nations. The Great Commission without a "nations" focus is missing its historic context and the place it holds in the mission of God.

When Jesus said *panta ta ethne* ("all the nations"), he redirected the mission and sent his people to the nations. God wants your church, my church, all of our churches, to go to and dwell in the uttermost parts as we join the mission. Depending on who counts and how they count, there are over six thousand unreached people groups. Three thousand of those are unengaged, unreached people groups, meaning there is little to no witness present.

Too often, Christians just seem to be interested in other things. I've noticed that when I blog about theological controversy, readers flock to my blog. And if I engage with dissenting comments, readers go crazy. But when I blog about the testimony of Christian missionaries in foreign contexts like Turkey, my readership drops significantly. It breaks my heart, because it is a reminder that people love theological controversies but not the nations.

The Nations in Your City

Most of us can't avoid the nations even where we presently live. God is moving people into our cities. Not all who will read this are from the United States, but many are. There is more ethnic diversity in the United States than in any country in the world. There are estimated to be 584 unengaged, unreached people groups in North America right now living in our cities.

God is moving people and groups into our cities and our neighborhoods. We can reach them without even getting on a plane. We need to send more who will go overseas, but we also need to preach the gospel and make disciples right here. The nations are waiting, sometimes next door.

At some point, somebody brought the gospel message to you. Now, we are the uttermost parts of the earth. It doesn't feel that way, but we are. Some will try to spiritualize Acts 1 and our failure to engage, saying, "Well, you know, this is my Jerusalem. I'm already in the Jerusalem God intended me to reach." But the truth is you really don't have a Jerusalem. That's not issued to you. Jerusalem is a city in Asia. Jerusalem didn't move to your hometown. Someone announced the gospel to you so that you might announce the gospel to others. Don't let your church be a cul-de-sac off the Great Commission highway.

WITH A MESSAGE: A GOSPEL-CENTERED FOCUS

The third commission of Jesus can remind us that the focus of the mission's message is gospel centered. Luke 24:46–48 says:

> He also said to them, "This is what is written: The Messiah would suffer and rise from the dead the third day, and repentance for forgiveness of sins would be proclaimed in His name to all the nations, beginning at Jerusalem. You are witnesses of these things."

Gospel centrality is important to clarify and define the mission. But sometimes theological phrases become clichés and lose their meaning. As theological terms are used in more contexts than originally intended, their meaning erodes over time. Before you know it, the semantic range is so vast that the term becomes ineffective. But it must not become so with *gospel centered*. The church needs to retain it in our missions vocabulary because repentance for forgiveness of sins proclaimed in his name to all nations clarifies the mission of God.

At the center of the gospel is the message of repentance. Ultimately the gospel is about a bloody cross and an empty tomb. Christians ought to "live sent" as ambassadors for Christ as they announce the bloody cross and empty tomb to all who will listen. We are sent to the nations with a message—and that message is one of repentance and forgiveness of sins, as this commission of Jesus clearly points.

Do you ever go somewhere and forget why you went in the first place? Recently I went upstairs, walked to my oldest daughter's room, and knocked on the door. "Come in," she said. I knew I came up there for a reason, but somewhere between the first floor and the second floor I forgot. So like a good father I just said, "I just want to tell you I love you."

It's easy to live sent and forget *why* you're sent. We would be naive at best, and reckless at worst, not to expect that many of us, even pastors reading this book, will fail to proclaim a clear gospel. You might say, "What a terrible thing to say." But we are no smarter and no better than the saints who went before us, those saints who faced the same pitfalls. And those traps snared them.

Throughout church history, we have been distracted by peripheral issues in ministry, when the gospel and its proclamation should and must be our focus. That also unites us in a gospel cause.

Diverse methodology in ministry is acceptable as long as gospel proclamation is clear. It doesn't matter so much if the congregation sings Isaac Watts or Israel Houghten. It doesn't matter so much if congregants wear suits or sandals, or whether they attend a house church or a mega-church. It does matter, however, if they miss this message of repentance necessary for reconciliation. A focus on gospel-centered mission helps the church move beyond stylistic differences. A faithful, biblical church that proclaims the gospel will look different in Singapore than it does in Senegal, different in Seattle, Washington, than it does in Selma, Alabama.

Now, this is hard for some seemingly theologically minded people. Let me illustrate with an unexpected occurrence happening in the "young, restless, Reformed" movement. Right now, it appears that African-American, theologically Reformed rap is popular. I didn't see that coming. Were any of you expecting that particular style of music to become generally accepted in the movement? Many are surprised because it is often the theologically minded people who want to point out those other approaches as wrong and worldly. They will speak of their "grave concerns." Have you heard that phrase? It is repeated time and time again throughout the blogosphere and in sermons regarding the methodologies of varying churches.

Then there's Lecrae. The reality is that, twenty to thirty years ago, many of the churches and the fellowships that we are a part of were preaching against the very kind of music ("methodology") Lecrae is doing. But because of the clarity of the gospel proclamation, approaches that were condemned then are affirmed now. What can this teach us? I want to encourage you to have a discerning but generous methodological view within a theological context because you're driven by the mission and more concerned about the gospel's proclamation.

You say, "Well, I was into that nations thing. I think it's great that they do that over there. But we don't have to contextualize over here." Really? God uses different kinds of churches to accomplish his agenda. God used the mega-church to reach Korea and the house church to reach China. There are marks of a church that should and must be true in every culture. But when the gospel is being preached, then churches on mission will look different depending on where God has sent them. Hold your models loosely and your gospel firmly, focusing on biblical marks. Gospel repentance and mission cause us to be gracious and loving as the gospel spreads. Gospel centrality also causes churches to become indigenous or rooted in their own culture as they remain focused on God's answer for man's need for repentance and our gracious God's saving grace.

Obviously, there is much more that could be said about specific methods. As you proclaim the gospel, and a church across your city does the same, it suddenly becomes apparent that you do so with differing ministries in your congregations. As God places us in unique contexts, we will lead unique ministries. It can be distracting and paralyzing if one decides to be the methodology mafia. Engage your city with the gospel, and celebrate those who do so as well.

One other issue that can distract from the message is that good deeds and gospel have been relatively pitted against each other. You simply cannot read the Scriptures and not be moved in word and in deed. You can't read the Scriptures and not care for the poor. But you should not be so naive as to read history and not see that those who emphasize serving the poor have often deemphasized the gospel. It is a horrible thing to say—unless you read history. But I believe this passage helps us to do gospel demonstration and gospel proclamation.

The message is that the Messiah would suffer and rise from the dead on the third day, and repentance for forgiveness of sins would be proclaimed in his name to all nations. It helps us to engage cultures. It helps us to serve the hurting. The church scattered cannot help but care for the hurting. Don't let anyone talk you out of that. We need more engagement, not less engagement, with the poor, the widow, the orphan, and the hurting. Jesus's ministry is linked to serving the hurting and demonstrating that to us.

In Luke 4 Jesus announces and inaugurates his public ministry, speaking about the poor, the marginalized, the sick, the hurting. In other places, he tells us to do the same, calling those who do "sheep" and those who don't "goats." Strong words. But the same Jesus who spoke the words of Luke 4:18–19 also said in Luke 19:10, "The Son of Man has come to seek and to save the lost."

It is this message that he's given us to so clearly proclaim. We can and must do justice. But it is not complete if we don't preach Jesus, and we can't preach Jesus and not care about justice. We need to live sent to the nations with a clear message.

EMPOWERED BY THE SPIRIT: A SPIRIT FOCUS

In Acts 1:6–8 we find the final commission of Jesus. In verse 6 Jesus is asked, "Lord, are You restoring the kingdom to Israel at this time?" At their question, Jesus kindly admonishes them, saying, "It is not for you to know times or periods that the Father has set by His own authority" (v. 7). They want to talk about the end times. Jesus wants to send them on a mission.

Churches are filled with people who are confused about the mission. It's evident when we consider what packs out a conference or what sermon series excites the people. For many churches today, when pastors address questions on the end times, the church fills up. If you pull out prophecy charts and some dragons with horns and start naming names and decoding the numbers, you can pack out a conference. Yet, Jesus says it's not for us to know. Jesus says no to the disciples' request to know the timing of God's plan, and he gives them something different entirely. He says, "But you will receive power when the Holy Spirit has come on you, and you will be My witnesses in Jerusalem, in all Judea and Samaria, and to the ends of the earth." These words cause a shift that takes place in the disciples' understanding of mission.

Luke's story of the church on mission in Acts begins with two revolutionary events. The first event focuses the mission of the church toward the nations and informs the disciples how the mission will be accomplished (Acts 1:8). The second creates the church and empowers it for its mission (Acts 2:1–11). When Jesus responds to his disciples' questions concerning when the kingdom of Israel will be restored (Acts 1:6), he is not trying to redirect their attention from eschatological speculation or from nationalistic hope in Israel's kingdom. Jesus says the kingdom will be established through the power of the Spirit, and the hope of Israel is fulfilled by God's mission being accomplished throughout the world.

We see a Trinitarian focus on the mission of God throughout Scripture. We see it in John 20:21–23:

> Jesus said to them again, "Peace to you! As the Father has sent Me, I also send you." After saying this, He breathed on them and said, "Receive the Holy Spirit. If you forgive the sins of any, they are forgiven them; if you retain the sins of any, they are retained."

Powerful Promise

Perhaps at this point in the chapter, you have this nagging concern: "All right, Ed, you talk about us living sent. So I need a congregation full of people who will quit being spiritual consumers and actually become missional co-laborers." This sort of shift is, in fact, a tall order. We know statistically, from a study we conducted of seven thousand churches in *Transformational Church*, that the majority of people in the majority of churches are unengaged in meaningful ministry and mission.[8] They will come for a show, but they won't serve.

---

[8] Ed Stetzer and Thom S. Rainer, *Transformational Church* (Nashville: Broadman, 2010).

So now you say, "You started with John 20:21. We are supposed to live as faithful missional co-laborers of the gospel, to live sent in our everyday lives. And then you tell me that now I've got to go to the nations, because, in context, the Great Commission cannot be understood apart from God's sending his people to the nations. How in the world am I going to do all these things?"

Well, first, you can't do all these things.

Second, remember the words of Jesus. He says, "You shall receive power when the Holy Spirit has come on you." You can't accomplish any of those things in your own power and strength. If the posture of mission is one of sent-ness, then the promise of mission is power from the Holy Spirit. You might not be able to accomplish all of your new ministry goals tomorrow. But one thing you can do today is to say, "Here I am, Lord; send me. Spirit, empower us. You've empowered us to live sent to our neighbors and to the nations."

The Way Forward

What should we do to focus on mission? I'd suggest that churches share Christ and serve the hurting locally, plant churches nationally, and adopt an unreached people group globally. I think you should lead your church to be a missional, missions-minded, gospel-centered, Spirit-empowered church.

Why?

They said at Babel, "Let us make a name for ourselves," so God scattered them. Their motivation was the exaltation of man's name. Israel was charged with a mission to bring the nations up to Jerusalem to praise God's name. In Acts the followers of Jesus praised God's name. In Revelation the heavenly host praises the Lamb. I desire our churches to be able to stand before God and say:

> Here I am, Lord; send me. Cause me to live as an agent of your mission, to partner with others to spread your gospel to the nations, because we love the nations. Cause me to proclaim the

gospel of repentance so that men and women might hear it all over the globe, by the power of your Spirit. In all these things, may we be a missional, missions-minded, gospel-centered, Spirit-empowered church.

When I look at the commissions of Jesus, I see a people that are commissioned. We're all sent. We're all to be missional Christians. But we can't get past the Great Commission without seeing the nations. We can't get past Luke 24 without seeing the centrality of the gospel. And we can't leave the commissions of Jesus saying we can do it on our own. *Spirit, give us your presence and your power.*

6
LET THE PEOPLES PRAISE YOU, O GOD! LET ALL THE PEOPLES PRAISE YOU!

John Piper

Psalm 67 is the focus for this final chapter. But before we begin, let me make two brief comments. First, Psalm 67 is the way we pray when we are besotted with God's zeal for his praise among all the peoples of the world. One of the barometers of the fruitfulness of this book is whether you are inclined to pray like this now more than before you began reading.

Second, one of the ways God alters the course of our lives is that when we hear a portion of God's Word, it takes root, and starts to grow, and doesn't wither. It hangs on. It revives again and again. It survives from season to season. It does something to us. We can't shake it. It holds us. It changes things. We can't fully explain it. But it becomes a call of God on our lives. May the Lord make Psalm 67 such a text for you.

Here's Psalm 67:

> May God be gracious to us and bless us
> and make his face to shine upon us,
> that your way may be known on earth,
> your saving power among all nations.
> Let the peoples praise you, O God;
> let all the peoples praise you!
> Let the nations be glad and sing for joy,
> for you judge the peoples with equity

> and guide the nations upon earth.
> Let the peoples praise you, O God;
>   let all the peoples praise you!
> The earth has yielded its increase;
>   God, our God, shall bless us.
> God shall bless us;
>   let all the ends of the earth fear him!

The way verses 1 and 2 relate to each other roots this psalm firmly in the way God is at work in history to save the world. Notice the connection between God's blessing Israel (that's the "us" of verse 1) and Israel's being a blessing to the nations (v. 2): "May God be gracious to us and *bless us* [note those words!] and make his face to shine upon us, *that* [this is the aim of God in blessing Israel] your way may be known on earth, your saving power among *all nations.*"

ROOTED IN GOD'S COVENANT

This connection between being blessed and being a blessing to the nations means that the psalmist is rooting his prayer in Genesis 12:2–3. God promises to Abraham, "I will make of you a great nation, and I will *bless* you and make your name great, so that you will *be a blessing.* I will *bless* those who bless you, and him who dishonors you I will curse, and *in you all the families of the earth shall be blessed.*"

So this prayer in Psalm 67 is not hanging in the air with no connections with God's historical way of saving the world. It is rooted in God's covenant with Abraham. It brings that covenant up to date and prays it into reality. That is what we are supposed to do with God's covenants—his promises. Bring them up to date and pray them into reality.

DECISIVELY FULFILLED IN JESUS

So let's do that—into the twenty-first century. I think the psalmist, and Abraham, would be upset with us if we didn't. The decisive fulfillment of God's covenant with Abraham—not the final fulfillment, but the decisive one—was the life and death and resurrection of Jesus Christ, the "seed of Abraham." And because Jesus in all his saving work is the seed of Abraham, everyone—including people from the most pagan nations—who is united to him by faith becomes a son of Abraham and an heir of all his blessings.

Galatians 3:13–14: "Christ redeemed us from the curse of the law by becoming a curse for us . . . so that in Christ Jesus the blessing of Abraham might come to the Gentiles [the nations!]." Galatians 3:7, 9, 29: "Know then that it is those of faith who are the sons of Abraham. . . . So then, those who are of faith are blessed along with Abraham, the man of faith. . . . If you are Christ's, then you are Abraham's offspring, heirs according to promise."

PSALM 67 IN THE TWENTY-FIRST CENTURY

So God's plan was that all the peoples of the world be blessed. To that end, he chose the people of Israel to bear his revelation and his blessing. And he made a covenant with them that they would be blessed and in that way bring that blessing to all the peoples of the world. And God fulfilled this covenant decisively when Jesus Christ, the seed of Abraham, fulfilled all righteousness and died for sin and rose again, so that anyone who believes on him from any people on earth will become a child of Abraham and inherit the blessing of Abraham—and so be blessed by the blessing of Israel. So the Abrahamic covenant is being fulfilled every time someone trusts Christ.

So we are going to read this prayer in Psalm 67 as part of the ongoing historical realization of this great covenant and its decisive fulfillment in Jesus and its ongoing fulfillment through the church. The prayer is really meant to be read as a realization of the covenant with Abraham and as an expression of how that covenant would be fulfilled in us today through Jesus Christ.

GOD'S GREAT PURPOSE FOR THE WORLD

The first thing we'll look at in the prayer is God's great purpose for the world and all its thousands of people groups. God inspired this prayer (which Jesus says about the Psalms in Matthew 22:43). And so we can see in it not just the *psalmist's* purpose, but *God's* great purpose for the world he made.

According to Psalm 67 God's purpose is to be *known* and *praised* and *enjoyed* and *feared* among all the peoples of the earth. This is why he created the world, why he chose Israel, why Christ died, and why missions exists—missions exists because the knowledge of God, the praise of God, the enjoyment of God, and the fear of God don't exist among the nations.

TO BE KNOWN, PRAISED, ENJOYED, AND FEARED

Let me point out each of these so you can see them for yourself.

1) God's purpose is to be *known* among all the nations. Verse 2: ". . . that your way may be *known* on earth, your saving power among all nations."
2) His purpose is to be *praised* among all the nations. Verse 3: "Let the peoples *praise* you, O God; let all the peoples *praise* you!" Verse 5: "Let the peoples *praise* you, O God; let all the peoples *praise* you!"
3) God's purpose is to be *enjoyed* among all the peoples. Verse 4: "Let the nations *be glad* and sing for joy."
4) His purpose is to be *feared*, or reverenced, among all the nations. Verse 7: "Let all the ends of the earth *fear* him!"

This psalmist is praying in accord with the will of God. That's what it means to speak "in the Spirit," as Jesus says the psalmists do. Therefore, we don't just see the purpose of a man in this prayer, but the purpose of God. His aim in this creation is that he be *known* and *praised* and *enjoyed* and *reverenced* among all the peoples of the earth. That's why the world exists. And that's why missions exists.

WHY THIS GREAT PURPOSE?

But the psalm tells us more about God's purpose for the world. It tells us what he aims to be *known* for, what he aims to be *praised* for, what it is about him that he means for all nations to *enjoy*, and why it is we should reverence him and *fear* to turn away from him to another god.

The psalm shows us four things that God wants the peoples of the world to *know* and *praise* and *enjoy* and *fear* about him.

First, God aims to be known as the one and only true and living God.

He is not the God of any other religion.

I gather this from the fact that an inspired Israelite poet is praying that *his* God will be known and praised among all the peoples who worship other gods. Verse 3: "Let the peoples praise *you*, O God; let all the peoples praise *you!*" The God of Israel said in Isaiah 45:5–6, "I am the LORD, and there is no other, besides me there is no God; I equip you, though you do not know me, that people may know, from the rising of the sun and from the west, that there is none besides me; I am the LORD, and there is no other."

If this is not true, missions would be the most audacious and presumptuous enterprise in the world. Calling the nations to know and praise and enjoy and fear one God alone, the God of Israel, the God and Father of our Lord Jesus Christ, would be arrogant and presumptuous, if it's not true that he's the one and only true God. But if it is true, then missions is a humble, daring, obedient response of a people who love those who are perishing.

The psalmist does not pray: May all the nations become sincere worshipers of their gods since all gods are one.

We Do Not Worship the Same God as Islam

And let's be crystal clear here: in a world supercharged with the presence of Islam, it does not help the cause of truth or love to say that we *worship* the same God—and I am putting the emphasis there on "worship." We do not worship the same God.

Muslims do not believe in a Jesus who died, who gave his life as a ransom, who rose from the dead, and who claimed to be the divine Son of God. All those things are rejected by Islam. The historical Jesus of the Gospels is denied by Muslims in at least those four critical ways.

What Jesus Says

And Jesus speaks clearly about people (of whatever religion— Christian or Muslim) who deny him in this way. He says:

> 1) *They do not "know" the true God.*
> You know neither me nor my Father. If you knew me, you would know my Father also. (John 8:19; see also 7:28; 14:7)

> 2) *They do not "honor" the true God.*
> Whoever does not honor the Son does not honor the Father who sent him. (John 5:23)

> 3) *They do not "love" the true God.*
> I know that you do not have the love of God within you. I have come in my Father's name, and you do not receive me. (John 5:42–43)

> 4) *They do not "have" the true God.*
> No one who denies the Son has the Father. Whoever confesses the Son has the Father also. (1 John 2:23)

> 5) *They have not "heard" or "learned" from the true God.*
> Everyone who has heard and learned from the Father comes to me. (John 6:45)

> 6) *They "reject" the true God.*
> The one who rejects me rejects him who sent me. (Luke 10:16)

Jesus's answer to the question is *no*. Neither Muslims, nor anyone else (in any religion, including Christianity), truly *worships* God if they reject Jesus as he really is in the Gospels.

Psalm 67 is praying that all the religions of the world, including Islam (which came into being perhaps sixteen hundred years after this psalm) would turn and know and praise and enjoy and fear the one and only true God—the God and Father of the

Messiah, Jesus. And Jesus endorsed this prayer with his own blood. He came into the world to awaken and save those who rejected him—like we all once did. Mark 2:17: "I came not to call the righteous, but sinners." So send I you (John 20:21)! He is sending out ambassadors today to all the Muslim peoples (and all the other religions), saying: *I love you, come to me and believe in my Son and I will give you life.* My purpose is to be known and praised and enjoyed and feared as the one true God—Jesus Christ.

So the first thing God wants the nations to know about him is that he is the one and only true God.

Second, he wants the nations to know that he is a God of justice.

Verse 4: "Let the nations be glad and sing for joy, for you *judge the peoples with equity.*" When the judgment of the nations comes, God will not be partial. No one will be condemned for the color of his skin, or the size of his brain, or the place of his birth, or the quality of his ancestry.

No bribes will be considered, no sophisticated plea bargaining. All will proceed on the basis of God's unimpeachable righteousness. Let this be known to all the peoples of the earth. They will stand on an equal footing with Israel when it comes to judgment. The standard of justice will be the same for both.

Universal Imperfection with Only One Remedy

And the standard of acceptance—his standard of vindication in the court of heaven—will be perfection. And the only remedy for our universal failure and rebellion is the *perfection of Jesus, which he performed* for all who believe in him, and the *punishment of Jesus, which he endured* for all who believe in him. Jesus's perfect obedience to God is not one remedy among others just for people in the Christian tribe. It is the only remedy for all the descendants of Adam. "As by the one man's disobedience the many were made sinners, so by the one man's obedience the many will be made righteous" (Rom. 5:19). If a person has embraced Christ as his only hope before God, he will be saved. If he has not, he will be lost.

And God will not be unjust toward those who have never heard the preaching of the gospel. They will not be judged for not believing in a Jesus they never heard of. They will be judged for how they have responded to the revelation they have. And Romans 1 tells us there will be no excuse (Rom. 1:18–21). None is righteous. None submits to God's truth outside Christ.

> The wrath of God is revealed from heaven against all ungodliness and unrighteousness of men, who by their unrighteousness suppress the truth. For what can be known about God is plain to them, because God has shown it to them. For his invisible attributes, namely, his eternal power and divine nature, have been clearly perceived, ever since the creation of the world, in the things that have been made. So they are without excuse. For although they knew God, they did not honor him as God or give thanks to him.

God aims to be known as a God of justice. The God of all the earth will do right. He will judge the peoples with equity—either in hell or in Jesus.

Third, God aims to be known for his sovereign power.

We see this in the last part of verse 4: "Let the nations be glad and sing for joy, for you judge the peoples with equity *and guide the nations upon earth.*" Many nations boast of their power and their independence as sovereign states. And when they do, the Lord laughs. Because he made the nations, he determined their allotted periods of time and the boundaries of their habitation (Acts 17:26).

"The king's heart is a stream of water in the hand of the LORD; he turns it wherever he will" (Prov. 21:1). "He removes kings and sets up kings" (Dan. 2:21). "He does according to his will among the host of heaven and among the inhabitants of the earth; and none can stay his hand, or say to him, 'What have you done?'" (Dan. 4:35).

They Will Hear

God aims to make himself known as supremely sovereign among all the nations—specifically that he runs the world. He is the guide of the nations. They are not sovereign. Only One is sovereign. And he sets the destiny of every nation.

And part of that destiny is that they hear the gospel. And to that end Jesus said,

> All authority in heaven and on earth has been given to me. Go therefore and make disciples of all nations. . . . And behold, I [I, the sovereign one with all authority] am with you always, to the end of the age. (Matt. 28:18–20)

My will is that the nations be discipled. All of them. And not only is this duty my will of command, but this destiny is my will of decree. "I will build my church!"

Fourth and finally, God aims to be known as a gracious God.

The only true God, who is just in all his judgment and sovereign in all his rule, is a God of grace. He wants to be known this way. We see this in verse 1: "May God be gracious to us and bless us and make his face to shine upon us, that your way may be known on earth, your saving power [literally, salvation] among all nations."

He aims to be known as a God who is *gracious* and who *saves*. And this doesn't mean "who is gracious only to Israel," because verse 4 says, "Let the *nations* be glad." If the grace of God were only for Israel, there would be no gladness for the nations.

Gospel: News of God's Grace

This is why the news that resounds through the world from the cross of Jesus on is called "gospel." It is good news. It is news of the God of grace. Paul said that with the coming of Christ into the world "the grace of God has appeared, bringing salvation for all people" (Titus 2:11). And when he summed up his life and ministry, he said it was all about the gospel of grace (Acts 20:24):

> I do not account my life of any value nor as precious to myself, if only I may finish my course and the ministry that I received from the Lord Jesus, to testify to the *gospel of the grace of God.*

The heart of the missionary message to the nations is: God will save you from your sin and guilt and condemnation by grace through faith in his Son Jesus Christ. We go with a message of grace, not a message of condemnation.

IN SUM

So to sum up what we've seen: God's great purpose in the world is to be known and praised and enjoyed and feared. And the truth about him that he wants to be known and praised and enjoyed and feared is

- he is the one and only true and living God, the Father of Jesus Christ;
- he is infinitely just and holy in all his ways, settling all accounts justly either on the cross for believers or in hell for those who reject his truth;
- he is sovereign over all the affairs of men and nations, and over the saving mission of his church through the all-authoritative, risen Christ;
- and he is a God of boundless grace to all who come to him through Jesus.

THE MISSION WILL BE FINISHED

Because he is gracious, he *aims* to be known among all the peoples. And because he is sovereign, he *will* be known among all the peoples. "I will build my church, and the gates of hell shall not prevail against it" (Matt. 16:18). "I have other sheep that are not of this fold. I *must* bring them also, and they *will* listen to my voice. So there will be one flock, one shepherd" (John 10:16). This gospel of the kingdom will be proclaimed throughout the whole world as a testimony to all nations" (Matt. 24:14).

This is the great hope and confidence that created the missionary movement of the Christian church. And this is the hope and confidence that will sustain us until we finish the mission. And it will be finished.

ONE FINAL POINT

There is one final point that needs to be made from Psalm 67—from the beginning and ending of this psalm. The psalm begins and ends with the connection between the people of God being blessed by God so that the nations will be blessed by us. We saw this in verses 1–2: "May God be gracious to us and bless us and make his face to shine upon us, *that* your way may be known on earth, your saving power among all nations."

What we have not noticed is that when the connection is repeated at the end of the psalm it is harvest time, and the blessing on the people of God is mainly a material blessing. Verses 6–7:

> The earth has yielded its increase [there has been a great
>   harvest—this is a harvest psalm],
> God, our God, shall bless us.
> God shall bless us;
>   let all the ends of the earth fear him!

So the immediate blessing in view is the way God has provided all the material needs of his people. "The earth has yielded its increase" (v. 6).

GOD IS WHAT MATTERS

And the amazing thing is that between the beginning blessing and the closing blessing in this psalm, the entire focus is not on material blessings for the world but spiritual ones—that is, God himself. Derek Kidner in his commentary says:

> If the setting of the psalm seems to be a festival of harvest home,
> it is remarkable . . . how nature is overshadowed by history, and
> the psalmist [is] stirred by hopes that have no material or self-

regarding element. . . . Here, nothing matters but man's need of God Himself.[1]

- Oh, Lord, let your way be known.
- Let our salvation be known.
- Let praise arise to you from all the peoples.
- Let joy overflow from the hearts of the nations.
- Show yourself a righteous judge, and a powerful guide.

The pervasive concern for the nations is that they would know and praise and enjoy and fear the true God—God himself.

Which means this, at least: God gives his people *material wealth* for the sake of the world's *spiritual worship*. That is, he blesses his church with riches for the sake of reaching the nations. He gives a bountiful wheat harvest for the sake of a bountiful world harvest. He gives us more money than we need so that we can meet the world's greatest need—the need to know God through Jesus Christ.

BLESSED TO BE A BLESSING

This is the sharpest point of this psalm. We are blessed to be a blessing. And, of course, that means we are spiritually blessed. But in this psalm, the Lord has something more specifically to say—especially to the American church and the church of the West.

I have blessed you—beyond the wildest dreams of any people in history. I have blessed you with unprecedented and overflowing wealth. This not a curse. It is a blessing. But it will become a curse if you do not use it for what I have designed.

BLESSINGS DOUBLED IN GOING AND GIVING

And what I have designed is not that you lose and they gain. What I have designed is that you go and you give, and *both* gain. I love you, and I love the nations. I have blessed you, and I mean to double your blessing by making you a blessing. It is more blessed

---

[1] Derek Kidner, *Psalms 1–72*, vol. 15 of Tyndale Old Testament Commentary (Downers Grove, IL: IVP Academic, 2008), 236.

to give than to receive (Acts 20:35). That's the way I created you. Therefore, my design ("blessed to be a blessing") is for your joy and their joy. When I bless you that you may be a blessing, I bless you that your joy may be full.

When I say, "Let the nations be glad!" I mean, "Let your gladness be doubled in their gladness." This is why I have blessed. This is why I have blessed you. Don't turn my blessing into a curse. Don't put it in a bag with holes. I have blessed you. This is why you are rich—"that my way may be known on earth, my saving power among all nations."

Let the peoples praise you, O God; let all the peoples praise you! Let the nations be glad and sing for joy.

For this we have been blessed. This is our mission. This is our joy. No matter what it costs.

A CONVERSATION WITH THE CONTRIBUTORS

David Platt, Michael Ramsden, Michael Oh, Ed Stetzer, John Piper, and David Mathis

The following is a lightly edited transcription of a panel discussion held on September 24, 2011, at the Desiring God National Conference, where the chapters of this book were originally delivered. David Mathis's questions are in bold.

How would you counsel someone wrestling through a possible missionary call? To what extent are there natural and supernatural factors that come into play as one would sense a missionary call to the nations?

Michael Oh: On one level, I believe that missions is not something that God invites us into. It's what we were saved for. And inasmuch as you are a Christian, you are called to that endeavor. But I do want to make a distinction between who is a missionary and who is not—who is a sender, who is a go-er. And toward that end, in terms of what it means to be one who goes, again, I think the first layer of missionary response or pursuit of that call is really the response of obedience. It flows from a passionate vision to see the name of Jesus Christ lifted high. And pursuing that call obediently and just hoping that God won't stop you in some way through your pastor or through circumstance or others and that God might just graciously, mercifully allow you to actually make it to the field, which is just such a hard thing to actually do. But I really do believe that it starts on the level of obedience and a passion for the things that God is passionate about.

David Platt: I would echo all of that and foundationally the missionary command that should supersede all of our lives. And in this sense I'd certainly understand and embrace much of what's being said in the distinction between go-er and sender. At the same time, I want to say to every member of our church that you're a go-er in the sense that you are going and making disciples. And we're doing this in all nations together. The question is where we're going and how long we're staying there. But we're all going in a very real sense. Even those who will stay in

Birmingham, I want us to make disciples in Birmingham with a view toward disciples' being made among the Arundo in North Africa. And I think about one brother who's here from our church who is making disciples in Birmingham. So he's still living there, but a couple from his small group is now leading one of our church planting teams among this dangerous, unreached people group in North Africa. And so he has been a part of making disciples in Birmingham, going in that sense that is then affecting unreached people. So that's what I mean when I say we're all to be involved in going, in some sense, to unreached peoples, because that's our end goal altogether. So there is the command, and then the call springs from that. And then it becomes an every-nation-to-every-nation thing such that everybody and every nation together, as followers of Christ, do this together.

And that he will. I'm always encouraged. And when we have folks that are praying, Is God calling me now to go and live somewhere else? I always encourage them, Just remember: the Lord wants his will and mission and purpose to be accomplished in your life more than you do. And as you abide in him, as you are totally surrendered to him, he will lead and guide and direct your steps. You go through the obedience of what God puts in front of you day by day by day by day. And trust that he is going to lead and guide those steps in a way that will make his glory known in wonderfully creative ways. I love watching the Lord take those that are obedient to that command and just play that out in so many different callings to so many different places in so many different ways.

Ed Stetzer: I have nothing to add but that there's a fundamental identification with being a believer, and that is we are sent. John 20:21 says, "As the Father has sent me, so send I you." But there are different ways that we're sent. We're all sent. There's a sent-ness that all believers are sent on mission. All believers are called to the ministry. We use these terms and we've got this special distinction. We say that, well, I was called to the ministry at a certain time. I'll often say between my junior and senior year in college. But 1 Peter 4:10 would say that each one has received a special gift. Use it to minister to one another as good stewards of the manifold grace of God. So I'm called to the ministry at my conversion. I'm sent on mission at my conversion. But then there are differences in where and among whom. And I think that's the distinction we would make.

I would say, Michael, since I think a good panel has a little bit of tension on it, I would say I would differ in one sense. I like the idea. I think we can look to the Great Commission and see the finishing of the task among the nations as a primary priority. But I don't like the emphasis on "get to the field." I would say that we're all in the field. The question has to be, to what field has God called us? And is it to the Pokot in Africa, the Quechua of the highlands of Peru or is it to Birmingham, Alabama.

So the nuance that I would make is that sent-ness is universal to the believer. We're all sent. The question is, Where and among whom are we sent to live, minister, send, and serve?

John Piper: Real practically, you do have to make some choices. And here's something that I just think God does over and over. Paul says in Romans 15, "Thus I make it my ambition to preach the gospel not where Christ has already been named, lest I build on someone else's foundation. But . . ." And then he quotes Isaiah. "'Those who have never been told of him will see, and those who have never heard will understand.' This is the reason why I so often have been hindered in coming to you."

Now here's my take on his understanding of that text in his life. He says that verse describes my life. That's why I do what I do. Well, no. He got knocked off his horse on the way to Damascus. That's why he does what he does. But, in fact, God takes the Bible and, with all the other things that happen to us, he burns a portion of it into you like he does nobody else. So one of the ways it gets specific—like deciding what field or when or at what age or whether I go to school—is you're reading your Bible and something happens. This verse takes you. It just takes you. You can't leave it. You try to leave it; it won't leave you. And so it's portions of the Scripture rooting in your soul and then over time being inescapable so that you can't leave it.

Very concretely, my departure from academia into the pastorate was the clearest decision I had to make, because most all the other decisions were made for me, it seemed like, but that one I really made. I really made that decision. I stayed up till one o'clock in the morning and I decided, and I was cornered by Romans 9. "I will be proclaimed not just analyzed." And I said okay. Okay. It took six years incrementally going, going, going, and then it just was like a strangle hold on me. And I just think God will do that for you. He will cause some portion of the Word to grip you, and it will be a decisive moment in your life.

Continuing on that practical note, what counsel would you have for someone who says God is uprooting him for world missions and asks, Where do I go from here? What does it look like from today, having made that decision to go, to getting to that new field and living sent in that new place?

Michael Ramsden: Not long after I became a Christian there was a very particular moment where I was confronted with the gospel and the reality of Christ, and I knew I had to surrender to him. And I went to my first Bible study four days later having read through the New Testament twice. I was halfway through the Old Testament. And we had this most amazing Bible study, and at the end they said, "If you could ask God one thing, what would it be?" And I said, "I want him to make me an evangelist. So if I could ask him one thing, that's what it would be. So would you pray that for me?" Now the reason why I'm saying that was that six years later I'm coming to the end of my doctoral research, which was on something called "systemic risk to financial markets," which I'm sure will be fascinating for all of you, for me to go into great depth at this point. And that was in '96. Yeah, '95/'96. And I was feeling pretty depressed because the conclusion of my research was that there was going to be a big collapse of the Western financial system. And I've had a lot of invitations from banks recently. And this guy Ravi Zacharias rang me up, and he said, "We think God's calling you to this kind of ministry. And if that's right, then would you like to join us?" Now you would think, given the first part of the story I shared with you, I would say this is an obvious decision and the answer's yes. It was not an easy decision.

Now my wife, who, generally speaking, is far more godly and righteous and holier than I am—she felt the answer to this was very simple. But for me it threw me into a tailspin. And I know. I spoke to countless leaders. Everywhere I went, I asked. I talked with people. I asked them to pray with me. And four months later I was preaching at a conference in Eastern Europe. I'd gone as a delegate and somehow got roped into preaching. One person said to me, "What are you thinking of doing next?" And I said, "Actually I have this big wrestle. Either I could go into banking or I could go into academia, or I've got this other offer on the table. I don't know which one to do." And I said, "It's not a question of obedience. If God would just send me a Post-It note—*Dear Michael, do this*—leave it on the fridge, and when I woke up in the morning, then that's it." And they just said, "Well, we really need Christians in banking. So our suggestion is, you're very young. You're only twenty-five. Why don't you say no to this offer and . . ."

So that morning I talked with the person and I thought, *Okay, that makes a lot of sense. That's what I'll do.* I didn't tell anyone what I was going to do. I went into my room later that day and I ran a bath and I got into it, and I broke down into tears and I cried for three hours. I don't know if you've ever cried to the point where you've run out of tears. It's actually very, very painful. But I just couldn't stop myself crying, and all I knew was that day I had made the single worst decision of my whole life. In other words, I got it wrong. And God instantly basically said *That's not the right answer. Why don't you try again.* And the words "Woe to me if I do not preach the gospel" took on a totally different meaning for me at that point.

And so I think the advice I would give is there's something that happens in the process of wrestling with that kind of decision, no matter where it is, whatever the field may be, whatever it may look like, and you must wrestle with the Lord in prayer. You must, I say, wrestle with godly people around you in prayer. Because there will come a time where you will either be tempted away from that calling or you will become hard.

And if you don't at that point know exactly what it is that you should be doing, the temptation will be to walk away. And that's why I think actually there are so few evangelists in the field, because times when, I think, it gets hard, they think there's something easier to do, and they go and do something else. So whatever that calling is, I will say you must wrestle with it. I was four years into doing what I'm doing, and I met with this financial group. And they said, "Michael, we're really interested in your research. We'll pay you thirty thousand dollars a day if you'll come and work for us." Now that's the kind of money that gets you to rethink your calling. And, yeah, I mean at that point I was making barely thirty thousand dollars a year. So thirty thousand dollars a day seemed . . . that was a significant pay rise. So I went home and I told my wife. I said, "Anna, I met with this group." And I had my deputy in the ministry with me at this lunchtime routine. And I said, "Here's the offer. What do you think?" So we started praying about it. And I think we prayed for twenty seconds and then we both fell about laughing. And we just stopped praying, and I said I know I'm not called to this. I'm called to what I'm doing now.

It's going to be hard. No matter where God has called you, no matter where he's placed you, there's going to be a time where it's going to be hard, and it's going to be difficult, and the temptation will be to walk away, or you'll be tempted by something else. And at that point you also need to know the certainty to what you have been called, that you're in obedience to God. And so I think you have to go through that wrestling process. So don't expect it to be easy. I think it's very rarely easy. I think there's that moment where you have to know that actually this is what it is and this is what it means. Now he may change that in ten years' time. That's fine. I think it needs to be clear. And I think so many of us drift into things. Now my belief in the sovereignty of God is such that I think God's more interested in getting us to the right place than we are in obeying him. But there is a difference between being in the right place and knowing you're in the right place, and being in the right place and not knowing you're in the right place. And if you're in the right place and you don't know you're in the right place, the danger is you'll end up somewhere else.

David Platt: I'm just thinking about all that wonderful process that God has ordained. Like he could, obviously, show it to you right now exactly what all this should look like, but he likely won't because there's a sanctifying process in the middle of it. So not to walk through that process alone but to walk through that process alongside a local church and a community of brothers and sisters and, ideally, elders or pastors who are helping shepherd you through that process and helping you think through what this is so you don't have to decide this on your own. That's part of the church. I mean that's part of the beauty of Acts 13. So worship and fast and pray with the church and with elders and leaders in the church and let them be a part of this process. And the Lord will use them to help guide those steps and direct those steps. That local church component, just like we heard last night, is just fundamental in this process and in sending you out and then supporting. I'm not just talking financially but in so many different ways that that's just key.

Michael Oh: Sometimes it is like John mentioned—a Scripture that burns in your heart. I think for me it was really "Love your enemies." And that was a clear kind of defining, clarifying Scripture for me to understand whether I should be going to China or Japan. And prior to that, however, it was just really a logical process. I knew . . . my wife and I knew. We needed—we were compelled—to be somewhere in the 10/40 Window. We wanted to be among the unreached, and there was a very logical process. Sometimes we can get paralyzed because we don't have that Sticky from God. And we sometimes can over-spiritualize a decision for future ministry and can kind of miss out on just the parts of humanity that God has given us. Like our logic and research, learning, and community to make decisions that are really not that hard. I mean, there's one missionary for every five hundred thousand Muslims in the world. That's a no-brainer. You should consider, for any of you feeling some call to mission, you should consider the Muslims. You should be compelled logically and in heart to consider the Muslims. And you should be compelled to pray for them, to be involved in some way no matter what your personal involvement will be. And for us it was kind of a narrowing-down process: the unreached 10/40 Window, feeling a call to Asia in terms of our backgrounds, and then crystallizing down to Japan. But I think even without that we could have ended up in Japan. And yeah, I'd just encourage you not to be paralyzed but to just move forward with all that God has given you, and use your minds. Use logic. And move forward as long as your conscience does not stop you or your leaders, and move forward with freedom in the gospel, freedom in the sovereignty of God, and he will lead. He will guide.

It might be helpful for some who aren't familiar with the vocabulary of missions if we ticked off a few key terms and had you give a brief definition or a sense of how those are being used. We're talking about nations, plural, and peoples, plural. What do we have in mind with that term?

David Platt: There are an estimated seventeen thousand people groups that Joshua Project and others—based on missiological, anthropological, and ethni-graphic research—identify as groups of people with common cultural language characteristics. So obviously when we see *ethnic* nations and peoples in Scripture, even nations in Matthew 28:19, this is obviously not going to be referring to nations as we would picture nations today. The United States of America, believe it or not, did not exist when Jesus said that, along with many other nations. And so when we see nations, it's talking about ethno-linguistic groups, groups that share these, and so this is where a variety of scholars have really helped clarify what these different peoples, who these different peoples are, and spread out. So India is one country, but people groups are everything— different languages, different culture characteristics. And those people groups are spread throughout the country. And they're here. They're here in the Twin Cities. You've got different people groups spread out throughout North America as well.

We talk about unreached and unengaged peoples. What do we mean by those categories?

David Platt: Unreached would be, on a whole, less than two percent evangelical Christian, and that's usually how unreached is defined. And so there's not a sustainable gospel presence, a large enough sustainable gospel presence really, in a people group for the access of the gospel. And that's key. When we talk unreached, what we're talking about is access, because I've heard people say, "Well, my neighbor's unreached in Birmingham." Well, they mean lost. Unreached doesn't mean lost; unreached means limited access, very little access. Just to put it practically, if you're born into an unreached people group, the likelihood is you would be born, you would live, and you would die without ever hearing the gospel. That's how it plays out. So that would be unreached.

Unengaged would be . . . you've got a people group that's not only unreached but there is no one intentionally targeting that people group to reach them with the gospel. And so you've got around three thousand, I think, people groups that would be unengaged and unreached.

What is "the 10/40 Window"?

Michael Oh: That would be ten degrees north latitude to forty degrees north latitude. Stretching from the East, Japan, China, Southeast Asia into North Africa and the Middle East where you have upwards of 95 percent of the unreached people groups of the world, where you have the greatest poverty in the world, and where you also tend to see the greatest persecution of the Christian church as well. And it's also an area where you have really some of the least engaged peoples and the least mission investment in terms of human and also financial resources.

What is "the Global South"?

Michael Ramsden: The globe is in two hemispheres. You have the northern bit, and then you have the southern bit. Again, some of these guys know this better than me, but it can be used in a variety of different ways. But the context in which you're most likely to come across it is the fact that the growth of the Christian faith and the spread of the church has been remarkable in terms of how it has shifted from the Northern Hemisphere to the Southern Hemisphere. That's been one of the remarkable stories. Even one of the leading books in this field was actually published through the Oxford University Press, just looking at that fact that now actually the church is that strong in these parts of the world now. Is there something more technical that I should add to that?

The one thing I would say, though, in terms of praying for the Global South is a lot of it has yet to be invaded by secularism. So one of the reasons why the country and the groups that I go to the most in South Africa is because its universities have bought into the North-Hemisphere worldview and they suddenly found evangelism more difficult. Now it's relatively easy to evangelize in South Africa compared to England. Okay. But if you compare South Africa to the rest of Africa it's actually become much more difficult. So these terms may have to be redefined at some point, but at the moment that's what we're basically talking about, this huge explosive growth in that part of the world. Is there anything more technical you want?

What do we mean by "contextualization" and "the C-Scale"?

Michael Ramsden: This is very noncontroversial.

Ed Stetzer: Contextualization is two thousand years of mission history, and we have more failures than we do successes in the area of contextualization. Contextualization has got a very good reputation among people who understand missiology. Some who use the term differently tend to think it's a terrible thing. But contextualization is not making the gospel palatable; it's making the gospel understandable, and there's an important distinction between the two. It's not giving people what they want, tickling their ears, if you will. It's not giving them what they want; it's giving them the gospel in the way they can understand, comprehend, and respond by grace and through faith to the gospel.

And so the question is, How far do you go? Now, the C-1 through 6 Scale was written by an anonymous author who was talking about Muslim contextualization. But many have appropriated that to other settings as well. But there's minimal contextualization, C-1, and it goes all the way till . . . C-6 is like a different category. It's essentially secret or hidden believers. Whereas, C-5 would be the place where the contextualization is, well, to the point where many of us—my work's in missiology—would probably see that as an over-contextualization. C-4 is where you're using local indigenous forms, cultural context is shaping. And the reality is in many ways of ministry the how of missions is going to be shaped by the who, when, and where of culture. But the question is how many. So the question is, How far is too far? And good, godly, Bible loving people disagree on where that line is.

I will tell you historically the vast majority of errors have been made on the side of under-contextualization in cross-cultural mission. We have had more danger with obscurantism, which is the technical term for when we obscure the truth of the gospel from those who are trying to see it through very different eyes. But the danger is, on the other hand, if the one hand is obscurantism, the other danger is syncretism—I'm quoting Dean Gilliland's book—but where we're impacted by paganism in its multiplicity of forms, and we concoct another gospel, that's not the gospel. So the danger is if you don't do contextualization you end up in obscurantism. If you do over-contextualization you end up in syncretism. And the attempt of the C-1 through do 6 Scale is to ask the question, Where is the sweet spot? Part of the challenge is that many of us want to sit back and sit out of the contextualization debate, and then say, oh, that's too much. And I think we want indigenous peoples to wrestle with this.

I was just in Brazil last month teaching a seminar in missiology and church planting there. And the Presbyterians there were asking these very questions. And it is better for them to wrestle through with that, with the Word of God, in conversation with others and other cultures in context. But it's very easy for us to sit back and say, well, no, you shouldn't do this or should do that. Ultimately we want the Word of God to shape, for them to interact, for them to wrestle with the Word of God and live it out in their own context. And that becomes an indigenous church. We hope that an indigenous church, East or West, young or old, springs up and uses the—I'm paraphrasing here—uses the forms from where it is. Ultimately that's what we want. And we all want that sweet spot where it's contextualized but not over-contextualized. That's what the scale is.

What is meant by the term *insider movement*?

Ed Stetzer: The insider movement is a debate, is a discussion, because an insider implies something, what inside what? Well, the phrase *Muslim background believers* is often used. But the insider movement would be the idea that you would stay inside of a Muslim context and thus be a follower of Isa, Jesus, be a follower of Isa within that. And the question then becomes, at what point do you break? I mean, you can't believe Islam and simultaneously believe that Jesus died on the cross for our sin in our place and God raised him from the dead on the third day.

Earlier this year I wrote the story for *Christianity Today* on basically . . . I called it "Proselytization in a Multi-Faith World." An odd title but I think *evangelism* is a uniquely Christian term. And my point in there is that, no, Islam and Christianity are not two paths to the same God. They're not two ideas. The idea is different. And so at some point you have to recognize that difference. But with insider movements the desire is in the deep-seated—and I so appreciate the desire to reach people without Christ in Muslim communities—that the gospel in their view would be shaped inside that Muslim context. And so in some cases they're still in the mosque, in the Muslim community, but at the same time they will be followers of Isa. And there are some pretty big theological, missiological debates about that, for obvious reasons.

As I mentioned earlier, on the contextualization scale the questions relate. On a contextualization scale C-5 would be where the insider movements would tend to be. I would be one who would affirm C-4 contextualization and recognize that the formation of new Christian communities, followers of The Way, who meet together as believers of Jesus Christ is part of the disciple-making process, and thus, I don't end up in the C-5 with the insider movement approach.

Moving on from the terms now, with five complementarians here who see the equal dignity and worth of men and women in God's image and differing in complementary roles for men and woman in the home and church, would you describe for us the very important place of single women in global missions?

John Piper: It's a really relevant question because 50 percent of the married people are women. Start there. And then there are very few single men but lots of single women. So put those two statistics together, the number of women on the mission field is huge. Seventy-eight percent, something like that? And a young woman over there was asking me between sessions about that. And I said we might address it here. I think there are, you know, reasons for that. But I'm not going to answer the question of what the socio-cultural reasons for that might be, but, rather, what's appropriate for them to do and what's the role. What the Bible calls for is men to lead the church and lead the home. Men should be the elders in the church, and men should be the head of their home. So then to extrapolate that onto the mission field would mean you look for roles corresponding to that. So I don't think it would be appropriate for a woman to be an elder on the mission field. I don't think it's inappropriate for her to fill all kinds of missionary roles that don't involve her in the role of an elder. And I don't think that would exclude evangelism, sharing her faith, and hundreds of other kinds of support roles. And so my guess is historically that the women who have, as singles especially, entered the mission force have been complementarians. They would have happily affirmed that when a church is formed here a man in this culture should take over, not that a woman in this culture should take over. And I would like to get behind that and try to make that happen. And

I'm sure that if a woman goes as a witness to her Lord, say as a nurse or as a teacher of English or just as an itinerant evangelist type, she's going to have these borderline ambiguous experiences where I wonder if what I'm doing right now is an elder-like experience. Like sharing the gospel in this village with men and women. And I think at those moments we should cut that a lot of slack and seek to say demeanor and disposition and theological orientation at that moment will make a big difference in whether she crosses the line and to do something that the Bible would find disobedient. So that's my take.

Michael Oh: In our city in Nagoya I would say the best missionary that I know, the most effective missionary that I know in Japan, is an older, single, female missionary, a wonderful, wonderful missionary and friend. And interestingly, the largest church in Nagoya was until recently led by a ninety-four-year-old female pastor. And one thing that I did say at Covenant Theological Seminary, when I was speaking there last year, is we can complain about what you may see as something that's biblically wrong in terms of the role of women in missions, but if you believe so strongly in that, you go. You go. You fill that pulpit. You stand up. You act on that conviction, and you go. And do it in a way that would honor God. So I think that there are men and pastors and seminary-trained guys who need to step it up before you complain about a woman doing something else.

John Piper: Or at the same time.

Help us think about short-term missions. What are their value, limitations, and dangers?

David Platt: I'm a huge believer in short-term missions done right. There are many abuses of short-term missions. When you think about short-term missions, talking about a trip into another context, often-times that goes awry on one of two levels. Either sometimes short-term missions actually hurts the work of the gospel in the field, which is detrimental, not good. And oftentimes it leaves people unchanged. So the people who are going—they go on a trip and they come back and it's been a nice trip, and they just kind of go on with their lives. Both of those— that's short-term missions done wrong. Short-term missions done right helps fuel long-term disciple making on a field. So that happens really through deep partnership with those who are serving alongside another context. So to have deep partnership with churches and ministry partners and mission partners who are doing long-term disciple making and have identified ways where a short-term team can help fuel a long-term disciple-making process can be hugely helpful for the spread of the gospel on the field.

And then it can be hugely helpful for those who are going. Part of our disciple-making process at Brook Hills, where I pastor, involves short-term missions. Short-term missions is a key component of our disciple making in Birmingham, because when I take a group of brothers overseas for a week or two, I can do more in their lives with the Word as they're seeing the world and we're serving alongside one another. I can do more in that week or two in their lives than I can in six months or a year sometimes in Birmingham where they're just choked out by all the stuff. And so they see it. They're changed. They're transformed. Some of our most effective ministry in Birmingham has been birthed through short-term missions in other contexts.

And then what happens is we challenge. Every year we challenge every member of our church to pray about giving two percent of their lives that year. So we challenge everybody to really pray and consider giving 2 percent of their lives the next year, which works out to about one week of their life, and we say to that 2 percent you go somewhere else. Two percent will radically transform the other 98 percent of your life that you live here. And so this has been one of the single-most important factors in really changing the climate in our church, because I think it's Word and world. All the seeds that I hope week by week that I'm pouring into them with the Word, they just soak in deep when they get into the world, and they begin to say, Oh, it makes sense. And then what happens is people start coming back and they say, you know, I'd rather spend 98 percent of my time there and come back for a 2 percent trip here every once in a while. And so then short-term ends up fueling midterm and long-term missions. So that kind of mission is done right. And then people see, wow, my life really can be part of God's global plan. And they begin to pray differently. They begin to give differently. Yeah. I think if we do it right, it can be an extremely helpful tool in the accomplishment of the Great Commission.

Ed Stetzer: I'm agreeing 100 percent. The key phrase is *if we do it right.* And you've done it right, and I appreciate so much what you guys are doing there in the Church at Brook Hills.

There is some research that tells us a lot of it's not done right. It's almost tourist missions. If you're actually involved in a zip-line tour when you're there on a mission trip, probably that's a bad sign. Bob Priest, one of my co-faculty members at Trinity Evangelical Divinity School, has done some of the best research on this and really has talked about doing it right. And part of the challenge is to help make those connections, to make those priorities, to come under and serve those who are on the field. Not to come demanding or saying, "I've got a group that needs to sing." You know, really, I don't need you to do that. Here's what I need you to do. But to say, "What can we do? How can we serve? How can we leave behind something positive?" But part of what we're trying to do is leave behind some connections. That's why short-term trips can often be a value.

One of the things I do in my ministry is intentionally go twice a year on short-term trips and partnership with the International Mission Board and something called the Upstream Collective. I bring pastors with me. And so we just returned from Central Asia. We've been to Taiwan, different places. I try to find pastors, maybe pastors here, church leaders here, who are not that engaged in God's global mission. And we bring them. I said, we just returned from Central Asia. To go to places and meet. And now it's been three months since we were in Central Asia. We now have three of those churches already in partnerships to plant churches in some major urban centers in Central Asia, working with incarnational missionaries who are there, but also working with indigenous believers. That's the kind of short-term missions trip I get passionate about, where it's not just go in, have a little touristy thing, have a little fun, make ourselves feel good. But really . . . well, and Central Asia is a long-term commitment. They're making a long-term commitment in a difficult field through short-term expressions along the way.

So I would just challenge you. If you haven't done that, I'll take you with me. And let's go see some of these connections and make some of these partnerships, because those relationships can make bridges—churches partnering with churches.

How would you counsel a layperson who is on fire for global missions but part of a church that is not?

David Platt: First of all, my encouragement would be to pray for your pastor, elders, to not do anything that would . . . you don't want to undermine the authority that God has put over you in a church. So that's fundamental. I hope that would be a given, but I want to make sure that that's clear.

The beauty, I think, of disciple making is that, and making disciples of all nations even, it's a grassroots picture. You don't have to have position or influence, so to speak, to make disciples. And so I would encourage you—and certainly be open; don't be hiding anything—to take a few people around you and say, How can we together be involved in praying for the nations and giving to the nations and going to the nations? And explore some opportunities. Start looking out there. Researching. What are some ways where I might be able to go on a short-term missions trip? And you lead it; you organize it or tag along with somebody else, like Ed was just talking about, and to go, and to do that with just a couple of people. And you think, *Well, but I want the whole church to do this or that.* But the Lord's not entrusted you at this point with that responsibility. And so be faithful with the responsibility he has entrusted. He's got people around you that you can mobilize for the spread of the gospel to unreached peoples. And so maximize that in a healthy submission to church leaders. But then my prayer is that as that passion begins to be infused to other brothers and sisters, that would result in some others beginning to mobilize others for missions. That would begin to infect a church in a really, really good way.

Michael Ramsden: It's a complex picture. If your pastor hasn't preached from the Bible, let's say, I don't know, the last year, you may want to consider how you fit within that. In North America, generally speaking, I imagine for most of you, you should be able to find a Bible-believing church where there is discipleship. So I agree with everything David said, I think, working on that assumption. Now, I think what does happen, and it may be even true for some pastors who are here, that we do get jaded, tired. You can lose focus. And then in which case you can be this huge blessing that I think David's talked about, by living in that kind of way and serving in that kind of way. And you just need to talk to any leader who's been in any leadership of any Christian organization or ministry or church for any period of time. There comes a time when you've dealt with so many different complaints and issues and so on, if someone comes to you with the wrong heart and attitude you can read that into them.So the act of serving can be a huge blessing.

At the same time, you could be in a church where you feel eventually that you will be opposed because of that. And I know that's unlikely in this particular group. But I've talked with university students, and one girl wanted to get together with two or three other girls in her church to pray for the people in their town that didn't know Christ, and the vicar in this case, Anglican vicar, said, "Well, I guess it wouldn't hurt anyone if you gathered and prayed." And then after a couple of months he decided he didn't like the fact that they were praying and asked them to stop. In which case that's probably time to leave. Is that okay? I don't want to cause any problems.

David Platt: It's okay with me. I was going to ask John a question along these lines. So we have people who come to Brook Hills from other churches in Birmingham. And I'm so against this flippant church hopping and shopping that is just this consumeristic picture in Birmingham when it comes to church. And so at the same time sometimes you get brothers and sisters who are coming who want to be sent long-term, and they don't see that potential in the church. So at what point would you counsel someone to consider moving churches with this passion just burning and it not being reflected? How do you counsel somebody in that situation? What point do they say, okay, maybe I need to make a change in the local body that I'm a part of?

John Piper: If they've over time done everything else that's been said here to awaken the church and the staff to a burden for missions and they're getting the message, the prayer support, the financial support, the community support for you is not here, that's serious enough biblical error and personal error to move and look for a place where you could find a base. I think that's a noble reason for looking. But I'm assuming they've tried. They've tried to love the flock where they were, and part of that love would be to awaken them to, I'd like this to be my home, I'd like this to be my base. Would you care for me? Would you send me? I should think even churches not interested in missions would often rise to that challenge. If you're our guy, our gal, you're here and you're asking us to be your base, your sending, it would be a pretty hard-hearted church to say no, we don't believe in that. But it does happen, whether it's blunt or not. And so, yeah, I think that's serious enough to go.

Ed Stetzer: John, let me follow up with a question on that, if I could. So if a church is teaching, preaching, we've done some of these other things but they're not having a passion for God's global mission, not involved in missions cross-culturally around the world . . . Since you've started asking questions across the panel, which I didn't know was allowed, I want to add one to that. So, John, I would wonder what if we have, as I think maybe we do often have in a theologically minded community, a lot of good teaching, perhaps strong expository preaching, perhaps even a desire to . . . and even with that church they're involved in global missions—so they're missions minded but they're not living, engaging their community around them. So it's a group of people who are, if you will, spiritual sponges. They sit, they soak, and they sour, but there's no intentionality to engage the local community, the community around, what we sometimes call our Jerusalem. But I would use that word cautiously. Is that a point to be concerned? Or is it if you're involved globally and you've got good Bible teaching, that's all you need? Or do you need to live on mission locally as well? At what point does that become a need to reconsider?

John Piper: The reasoning there would be a little different, but they're related. The reasoning there would be different because you don't need the church's financial support to be a faithful witness in your neighborhood. Where it might overlap is what you want to reach people for is to fold them into a body of Christ. And you want to fold them into a healthy body of Christ that has a burden for lost people. And then your question becomes, is this a place where they can be discipled? And if you conclude the lack of seriousness about the faith means, I don't think I'd bring a baby believer here, then you're in a similar kind of situation, I think.

It's a great comfort that Jesus ends the Commission with the promise to be with us. As we close, is there a word of hope that you would have to help strengthen men and women serving in difficult missionary contexts, in particular cross-cultural situations?

John Piper: The story of John Paton brings tears to my eyes. Not just when he said good-bye to his dad. That's a real tearjerker, if you have sons. But the story on Tanna when he had given, what, two or three years of his life to these savages, who ate the missionaries who were there just before him. And he gave it his best, and they mounted a move against him. And he's fleeing for his life with several thousand natives chasing him in the New Hebrides. And the guy who's, I think his name is Abraham, trying to help him escape said, "You go up this tree and I'll divert them over there, and then you come down. You'll get away to another island." And he said, "I sat in that tree"—he's telling the story now forty years later—"I sat in that tree, and I would not trade the sweetness of the fellowship of Jesus in the promise 'I am with you to the end of the age.'" And I just think whatever your situation, you can't get much worse than that, I don't think, is when you're about to be killed and they're just below you. If they look up, you're dead. And you are experiencing the fellowship of the living Christ at such a level that forty years later you say I wouldn't have traded it for anything. Louie Giglio, if you lost your fellowship with Jesus, it could be he's on his mission over here and you stayed here. So I really believe there are good Christian-hedonist reasons for being a missionary, mainly that God keeps his best wine in the cellar of suffering. I didn't make that up. That's from the Scottish guy, whatever his name is. And there's plenty of suffering out there to go around for everybody. But if you go into missions, God has given the go-ers . . . he's given the go-ers—whether it's local go-ers or far away go-ers—he's given them the kind of assurances that I think he delights to sweeten the fellowship that he has with the go-ers because they're doing something so close to his heart, and they come into crises where that particular promise "I got all authority" and "I'm going to be with you." We experience that more deeply, more preciously, more sweetly, in the laying out of our lives for others than at any other time.

Ed Stetzer: It's not just that Jesus promises his presence in Matthew 28. Every time Jesus gives in what we see the four major commissions, every time there's a promise. In John 20:21 he speaks peace twice—not once but twice. "My peace be with you." In Matthew 28 he gives the promise of his presence. In Luke 24:46–48 we see the ongoing presence, the peace there. And in Acts 1:8 he says the Spirit will come upon you and you will be witnesses. So there's a recurring theme. We do not go alone. We do not go unempowered. We do not go without the grace and the understanding and the peace that passes all understanding. And I think then we understand why people can with such joy be on the top of a tree facing death, why people can with such joy be, as the Scripture says, sewn in half. Why? Because in the midst of that moment when we're living on mission for the gospel we know that he is there, his peace is there, his Spirit is there. And that makes everything worthwhile.

David Platt: One of the things South Sudanese brothers and sisters have taught me through twenty years of civil war and persecution and having helicopter gun ships come through their villages and wives and daughters raped and all of this, to go to those brothers and sisters after twenty years of civil war and the words that continually come out of their mouths, they just continually say, "God is greater. Our God is greater." And they smile just big Sudanese smiles when they say, "Our God is greater." And so to say to those who would be in the circumstance, whether here or watching, greater is the One who is with you than the one who is in the world.

And we've got a couple that we sent out to this really difficult people group in North Africa. The last five couples that have gone to work in this assignment have all for very weird, strange reasons had to leave. They all experienced tragedy or different things. And so we knew that going in. And they experienced something weird over the last couple of weeks health wise, where they didn't know what was going to happen. And just to say to them, Don't forget the One who is in you is greater than the one who is in the world.

Michael Ramsden: Could I maybe add something a little different to the question? I think it may be related. It could well be that there are some of you who are here and your question is, Well, how can I be meaningfully involved? We sometimes talk about God plus one is a majority, and we use phrases like that, but it seems very abstract. And I would like to encourage you that no matter how small it may seem to you, what God is asking you to do, or however insignificant, you may have no idea what that may actually mean or come to.

Over the last few years I got to know a guy called John Bechtel, who used to be with the DeMoss Foundation. They used to do a lot of work into China. And he is in his late sixties, maybe early seventies now. They were involved in having the Bible broadcast at dictation speed into China after everybody was thrown out. As a matter of fact, his family was the last missionary family expelled from mainland China when everything came down. His father's theological library was piled outside his study. They set fire to it. He was a young boy at the time, and he got shipped over to Hong Kong, and they got physically thrown out of the country. And anyway, he was educated at that point, and he was desperate. John felt a strong call to go back into China. That was absolutely impossible. There was just no way in. They looked every way they could to get back in, and he began to look in Hong Kong. And the Lord laid it on his heart to start an orphanage. And because he'd been educated in England and obviously he was living in a former British colony—I guess we're in a former British colony now—but anyway, he was living in a former British colony, and he suddenly realized that the governor of Hong Kong, they'd been in the same school together. So he thought, *Well, this will be easy. I'll go to the governor and we'll share old school stories together. We're in the same class for seven years. And then I'll say, Hey, can you give me some land? I want to build an orphanage.* So he had dinner with the governor, and then he said, "Hey, I want to do this." And the governor said no. So he looked at various other avenues, and the answer was no.

And then he was walking through a certain part of Hong Kong, and he saw a school that had been built and it was closed. There was a for-sale sign outside. He thought, *This is perfect. I could buy this.* And he started writing around, again, to all the people he knew in Hong Kong. This is back in the sixties. He couldn't really raise any money. No one was interested. An American friend of his was visiting and said, "Look. This is crazy. This seems like a perfect thing. Come to the States. We'll arrange a preaching tour for you. And I'm sure you'll get all the money that you will need to buy this building." And John prayed about it and he was sure that that was the right word. He went and he preached. He came to Hong Kong, and a month later he got a brown envelope. And he opened it up, and inside was another envelope with a letter from his friend. And his friend said, "John, out of all the churches you preached and everyone you went we've only received one gift." Okay? And it's in this one letter. And he opened up the letter, and it was a letter from a twelve-year-old girl, who'd been saving up her allowance and had finally saved one dollar. And she had written a small note saying, I would like to give this one dollar for the purchase of this orphanage, and signed her name, and that was it.

And John describes how he was utterly heartbroken. But as he prayed about it, he thought he would go to the caretaker of this building. And he went and he rang the bell, and the guy came to the iron gates and he said, "I would like you to pass this offer to the owners of this building for me to purchase it." And handed this letter, this note from a twelve-year-old girl with a dollar bill in it. And the guy laughed at him and threw it out. Now, if you know John he speaks fluent Mandarin and Cantonese. And so he let it be known in no uncertain terms that if the caretaker refused to pass on this legitimate offer to the owners of the building, he'll take him to court for breach of contract law and in violation of the regulations concerning the sale of buildings in Hong Kong. So the caretaker said fine. A week later he gets contacted by the owners of the building. And they said, "We've read that little girl's letter. And we are so touched we will agree to sell this building to you for one dollar."

Twenty-five years later John was preaching in North America and he told this story, and a woman in her thirties at the end came up to the front and said, "I was that girl. That was my dollar I sent you." And he ran back out into the car parking lot and tried to call as many people who had been leaving the sanctuary back in and introduced them to this woman who had been one of the illustrations in his sermon. Now that one dollar that she gave, that was everything she had. She gave everything. And she never knew the outcome of that story until later, because there was no address. There was just this handwritten letter with her name at the bottom. So the church took up a collection. I think they raised fifty thousand dollars, which was more than enough to buy her an air ticket to Hong Kong. So she went to Hong Kong and made a cash donation for an extension of that orphanage. One dollar.

So it may be if you're sitting here and you're feeling discouraged and you think, well, look, God is . . . it's just such a little thing he's given me, you may have no idea how when that's placed into the hands of God what that may actually do and the effect that that may go on to have. And so I would urge you to give. I was astounded by the way the eight-and-a-half thousand dollars got the Arabic website for John Piper up. There's a group of people in this room who need to write a check for eighty-five thousand dollars, because that project's far too small and insignificant. I'm sure it should be fully funded by now at least four times over. So it should be eighty-five, and it should be much bigger than that. But I wish we could all learn from this girl and just give more generously.

You know, in England one of our pound coins has a picture of the queen on it? She's our head of state. And if any of you want to end your mindless rebellion and rejoin the motherland, we're happy to welcome you back. And in England we sometimes say we hold onto our pound coins so tightly we make the queen cry. So be generous with what you have. And you may be amazed what God will do with it. You may not know what he's done with it until the other side of eternity, but he can use you in surprising ways.

John, would you close this panel in prayer?

John Piper: Father, we cast our bread on the water, and I pray that you would cause it to feed, and I pray that it would come back. And I pray, Oh God, that you would be doing among every person the unique work that you appointed for this conference. And it is unique. May none compare him- or herself with another. May they deal straight with you about what you might be doing in their lives financially, vocationally, in the family, in the church, in the soul. God, do extraordinary, Christ-exalting, church-strengthening, nations-reaching things. And now, Lord, give us the respite we need here in the next minutes and bring us back together here this evening. We pray in Jesus's name. Amen.

APPENDIX

What Next? Disciple a Few

David Mathis

You then, my child, be strengthened by the grace that is in Christ Jesus, and what you have heard from me in the presence of many witnesses entrust to faithful men who will be able to teach others also. Share in suffering as a good soldier of Christ Jesus. No soldier gets entangled in civilian pursuits, since his aim is to please the one who enlisted him. An athlete is not crowned unless he competes according to the rules. It is the hard-working farmer who ought to have the first share of the crops. Think over what I say, for the Lord will give you understanding in everything.

—2 Timothy 2:1–7

Now what?

Maybe you attended a missions conference. Or heard a life-altering message. Or read a missions book like this one—and maybe it was just a single chapter or paragraph, even a single sentence, that set you on fire for joining in God's global mission. Or perhaps, best of all, you were turned upside down by personal interaction with a fellow Christian.

Maybe for the first time, you're seeing that we are all "sent." Every Christian is called to live on gospel mission. Whether God is doing an unprecedented work in you for "living sent" where you already are or calling you to cross a culture in missions, what's next? Where do you go from here?

WHERE TO FROM HERE?

Here's the guidance David Platt has for us in his book *Radical*:

> I am concerned about a general vagueness that has existed in contemporary Christianity regarding the next step. We have seen

that God blesses us so that his glory might be made known in all nations. But an all-important question remains. *How* do we make God's glory known in all nations? If God has given us his grace so that we might take his gospel to the ends of the earth, then *how* do we do that? Do we walk out into the streets and just start proclaiming the glory of God somehow? Should we all go to other nations? If we go, what do we do when we get there? What does all this look like in our day-to-day lives?

Jesus has much to teach us here. If we were left to ourselves with the task of taking the gospel to the world, we would immediately begin planning innovative strategies and plotting elaborate schemes. We would organize conventions, develop programs, and create foundations. We would get the biggest names to draw the biggest crowds to the biggest events. We would start megachurches and host megaconferences. We would do . . . well, we would do what we are doing today.

But Jesus is so different from us. With the task of taking the gospel to the world, he wandered through the streets and byways of Israel looking for a few men. Don't misunderstand me—Jesus was anything but casual about his mission. He was initiating a revolution, but his revolution would not revolve around the masses or the multitudes. Instead it would revolve around a few men. It would not revolve around garnering a certain position. Instead it would revolve around choosing a few people. He would intentionally shun titles, labels, plaudits, and popularity in his plan to turn the course of history upside down. All he wanted was a few men who would think as he did, love as he did, see as he did, teach as he did, and serve as he did. All he needed was to revolutionize the hearts of a few, and they would impact the world.[1]

IF BILLY GRAHAM HAD BEEN A PASTOR

Billy Graham once was asked, "If you were a pastor of a large church in a principal city, what would be your plan of action?"

In the modern-day classic *The Master Plan of Evangelism* (which has gone through over one hundred printings since it was first published in 1963), Robert Coleman reproduces Graham's response, perhaps a surprising answer to many:

---

[1] David Platt, *Radical: Taking Back Your Faith from the American Dream* (Colorado Springs, CO: Multnomah, 2010), 87–88.

I think one of the first things I would do would be to get a small group of eight or ten or twelve people around me that would meet a few hours a week and pay the price! It would cost them something in time and effort. I would share with them everything I have, over a period of years. Then I would actually have twelve ministers among the laypeople who in turn could take eight or ten or twelve more and teach them. I know one or two churches that are doing that, and it is revolutionizing the church. Christ, I think, set the pattern. He spent most of his time with twelve men. He didn't spend it with a great crowd. In fact, every time he had a great crowd it seems to me that there weren't too many results. The great results, it seems to me, came in this personal interview and in the time he spent with his twelve.[2]

THE GRUNT WORK OF THE GOSPEL

Second Timothy 2:1–7 is one such summons to paying the price. It's a call for blue-collar Christianity—for rolling up your sleeves, putting on your mud boots, and doing the grunt work that moves the gospel forward. In particular, verse 2 is a pointed challenge from the apostle Paul to his disciple Timothy, and to us, to invest our everyday lives in the typically underappreciated, under-celebrated, often menial and thankless work of giving our lives in depth to a few individuals for the sake of their growth and joy and the advancement in the faith and the multiplying of their lives in others also.

"The grunt work of the gospel" is the labor of cold, hard disciple making. There are very few frills. Rare accolades. Low hype. It's jolly hard work that doesn't grab headlines or come off as fascinating to the masses. And so this appendix, in keeping with the text of 2 Timothy 2:1–7, is a summons for engaging in the grunt work of gospel advance through personal, intentional, relational, patient, gospel-centered disciple making. First, we'll look at 2 Timothy 2:2 and the call for making disciples. Second, we'll look more broadly at the context and see how verse 2 relates in particular to what follows. Third and finally, we'll end with where

---

[2] Robert E. Coleman, *The Master Plan of Evangelism* (Grand Rapids, MI: Revell, 1993), 103.

we find the strength for giving our lives to the necessary but typically no-recognition work of making disciples.

1) CHRISTIANS ARE CALLED TO MAKE DISCIPLES WHO MAKE DISCIPLES (V. 2)

Verse 2: "And what you have heard from me in the presence of many witnesses entrust to faithful men who will be able to teach others also." Here Paul is calling Timothy, and with him implicitly Christians today, to what we might call "disciple making," to use the language of Jesus's Great Commission. The word *disciple* simply means "learner" or "follower" or "student." For the Christian, the idea of discipleship and disciple making comes from the life of Jesus. For over three years, Jesus mainly trained twelve men who were his "disciples," his round-the-clock followers—the students of his whole life, not just the masses he addressed in bulk. The disciples spent countless hours with their mentor, not only hearing him teach in public but traveling with him, eating with him, doing all of life with him.

"Disciple" does not mean that they learned only in the classroom. Jesus didn't have classrooms like we think of. The world was his classroom. Everyday life was his classroom. And his disciples weren't mere learners of information but learners of Jesus's whole life. And following Jesus's example, Christian disciple making is about intentionally and relationally investing oneself in the spiritual growth and maturity of a few disciples—part of which is training those disciples to then disciple others who disciple others. The way Paul says it in 2 Timothy 2:2 is that Timothy should *entrust* what he's heard from Paul to *faithful men* who will in turn do the same for *others also*.

So, under this first heading "Christians are called to make disciples who make disciples," let's note from verse 2, and its context, what is meant by the kind of disciple making that Paul modeled and is calling Timothy to—and us to. There are at least three important aspects here to disciple making: intent, context, and content.

First, the intent. Disciple making demands intentionality. This intentionality, or plan for multiplication, is what makes 2 Timothy 2:2 such a memorable verse—it's the generational awareness and pregnant phrase "others also" at the end. "Entrust to faithful men who will be able to teach others also." Paul's charge to Timothy is not only that he be a disciple—and not only that he make disciples—but that he make disciples who make disciples. It's generational thinking, a strategy for gospel multiplication, not mere addition. It involves seeing and investing in disciples not only as ends in themselves but also as means to making other disciples, who then make disciples.

Note that Paul explicitly mentions four generations in verse 2: Paul himself, Timothy, the faithful men, and the others also— and implicit in "others also" is the ongoing transmission to spiritual generation after generation. Disciple making involves being intentional in personally mentoring another believer, or a few, younger in the faith (though not necessarily in age), not only to be a disciple himself but then to turn and invest in others, such that he also makes disciples who make disciples. But there's not only intentionality here, with a strategy for multiplication. Intentionality on its own will become cold and calculated.

The second aspect of disciple making to notice here is the context: deep relationship. Disciple making is not an event (like new birth), but a process (like sanctification). Where this deeply relational dynamic of disciple making comes out so strongly in this text is Paul's relationship with Timothy. In verse 1 Paul calls Timothy "my child." Back in chapter 1, verse 2, he calls him "my beloved child." And in 1 Timothy 1:2, he called Timothy "my true child in the faith" and again in 1 Timothy 1:18, "my child."[3]

This is affectionate, familial language reflective of an intimate and deep relationship. Paul's discipling of Timothy was not mere formal information transfer. It was not a professor-student classroom interchange. It was not held together merely by inten-

---

[3] Paul also calls his disciple Titus "my true child in a common faith" in Titus 1:4.

tionality and multiplication strategy and training Timothy to train others. But the context for Paul's disciple making was profoundly relational. He deeply knew Timothy. Whenever possible, they did life together. There must have been both quantity and quality time. There was a deep love for and enjoyment of each other, such that Paul says in 2 Timothy 1:4, "I long to see you, that I may be filled with joy." And this comingling of intentionality and relationship made Timothy a kind of spiritual son to Paul, which really illumines the discipling relationship. Disciple making is a kind of spiritual parenting.

As a brief aside here, the call to disciple making begins in our homes. It begins with being intentional and relational in caring for and leading our wife and being concerned for her spiritual growth and well-being, and in exercising the discipler's mindset toward our children. I do believe God is calling us here in 2 Timothy 2:2 to intentional and relational investment, a kind of spiritual parenting, in a few specific others outside our homes. But don't think for a minute that it ever means anything less than disciple making in our own homes—or to the detriment of disciple making in our homes. Disciple Making 101 is caring for and nurturing and growing—*discipling*—our families. *And* it's not the only thing included in disciple making. God also calls us to invest ourselves in the lives of spiritual children, outside our home. But it starts in the home, as it did for Timothy.[4]

So spiritual parenting, seen in Paul's affectionate language to Timothy, is a help for us in thinking about the dynamic of intentionality and relationality. But there is one more essential dynamic at work here in 2 Timothy 2:2. There is not only intent and context, but also content.

Third, the content of disciple making centers on the gospel. Here let's quickly make the case that the phrase "What you heard

---

[4]Note elsewhere in 2 Timothy how Paul acknowledges that Timothy's own discipleship started in the home. In 2 Timothy 1:5 Paul says that Timothy's faith "dwelt first in your grandmother Lois and your mother Eunice," and he notes in 3:15 "how from childhood you have been acquainted with the sacred writings, which are able to make you wise for salvation through faith in Christ Jesus."

from me in the presence of many witnesses" refers essentially to the central message of the Christian faith, namely, the gospel that Jesus saves sinners. Note the word "entrust": In 1 Timothy 1:10-11 Paul says that "sound doctrine" is that which is "in accordance with the gospel of the glory of the blessed God with which I have been *entrusted*." So Paul says that he has been "entrusted" with the gospel. Then seven verses later, in 1 Timothy 1:18, he says, "This charge I *entrust* to you, Timothy, my child." And at the end of 1 Timothy, in 6:20, he writes: "O Timothy, guard the deposit *entrusted* to you."

So here's what we have so far: Paul has been "entrusted" with the gospel; and now he is entrusting this gospel, which he also calls "the deposit," to Timothy. This is where Paul ends 1 Timothy, and where he goes right away in 2 Timothy. In 2 Timothy 1:12 he refers again to the gospel as being "what has been *entrusted* to me," and then in verse 13 he turns to Timothy and tells him, "Follow the pattern of the sound words that," notice this phrase, "*you have heard from me*." Sound familiar? It's the same wording as 2 Timothy 2:2: "What *you have heard from me* in the presence of many witnesses entrust to faithful men."

Then in 2 Timothy 1:14 Paul charges Timothy to "guard the good deposit entrusted to you" (here's the "deposit" and "entrusted" language together). So what's happening in 1 Timothy and then in the first chapter of 2 Timothy is that Paul is reminding Timothy that in discipling him he has entrusted to him the gospel, which he also calls what "you have heard from me" in verse 13 and "the deposit" in verse 14. And Paul charges Timothy to guard it (v. 14) and to live it out (v. 13).

But then something new and very significant happens in 2 Timothy 2:2. In 1:13–14 Paul merely said to guard it and live it out, but now he says *entrust it to others*. Don't only guard it and live it out (don't just be a disciple) but pass it along (make disciples)—and do so in such a way that they make disciples as well (make disciples who make disciples). Build the gospel into them. Be intentional and relational. Be personal and particular and patient. Entrust the treasure of the gospel into other jars of clay (2 Cor. 4:7)—in a process, not an event—at such depth and potency that they can't help but then spend their lives building the deposit of the gospel intentionally and relationally into others.

It is the gospel that is the message that Timothy heard from Paul "in the presence of many witnesses."[5] And so when he charges his disciple in 2 Timothy 2:2 to turn and make disciples who make disciples, he's not referring to their backroom conversations or his own personal hobbyhorses or idiosyncrasies, but the main things, the things Timothy heard from Paul again and again, "the sound doctrine" centered in the gospel of Jesus giving himself at the cross to save sinners like us.

So the call to disciple making here has at least these three aspects: (1) intentionality, (2) relationality, and (3) gospel-centrality.

Why This Applies beyond Timothy

Now briefly, before we touch on verses 3–7, here's why the 2 Timothy 2:2 summons to disciple making applies not only to Timothy but to all Christians. When Paul appeals to Timothy to engage in the grunt work of disciple making, he does not do so because Timothy is some kind of special apostolic delegate or has some unique gifting. There is nothing special or irreplaceable about Timothy. Rather, three times in the span of just a few verses, Paul appeals to universal truths about any healthy Christian in his call for disciple making. In 1:13 he tells Timothy to follow his pattern of sounds words "in the faith and love that are in Christ Jesus." In 1:14 he says Timothy should guard the gospel "by the Holy Spirit who dwells within *us* [and note the plural here!]." Then in 2:1 he tells him to be strong "in the grace that is in Christ Jesus." Three things true of all Christians. So

---

[5] Note here that there is a community context for disciple making. It's not Paul and Timothy locked away in a room. It happens in the everyday life of the church and alongside the public proclamation of the gospel ("in the presence of many witnesses"). Sermons, books, blogs, classes, and conferences play an important role in disciple making, but they simply do not replace the heart of relational, intentional, gospel entrusting.

Paul appeals to universal Christian realities—faith and love in Jesus, Holy Spirit indwelling, and grace in Jesus—not to something special or unique to Timothy, when he instructs Timothy in verse 2—and thus with him, all Christians—to make disciples who make disciples.

2) DISCIPLE MAKING IS HARD WORK AND BRINGS SUFFERING (VV. 3–7)

Here's where we put on the blue collar, get down in the trenches, roll up our sleeves, and talk about the grunt work. While we have this pristine, ideal, undiluted picture of disciple making in verse 2, we find a surprising reality coupled with it in verse 3: suffering. Don't miss this: Paul has bookended this section to Timothy on gospel transmission with the same phrase "share in suffering" in 1:8, and then again in 2:3. This whole passage is about Timothy's sharing in Paul's suffering by joining Paul in his mission of gospel advance through disciple making.

In verses 4–6 Paul then develops the charge to Timothy to share in suffering, again right on the heels of verse 2, with illustrations of single-mindedness (the soldier), discipline (the athlete), and hard work (the farmer).

Single-mindedness. Verse 4: "No soldier gets entangled in civilian pursuits, since his aim is to please the one who enlisted him." Satan has a thousand readymade, often event-oriented distractions to divert us from pleasing Jesus in the grunt work of advancing the gospel through the process of disciplemaking.

Discipline. Verse 5: "An athlete is not crowned unless he competes according to the rules." Disciple making often feels like a really long lap around the stadium. It would be so much easier to take a shortcut across the field. There is great temptation to cut corners by constructing mechanism after mechanism, and program after program, for mass-producing disciples. But disciples who make disciples can't be mass-produced. I've seen it again and again, where Christians made by event after event, but not coupled with intentional, relational, gospel-centered disciple making, go haywire at the strangest times. Defaulting to the easier, often more single-event, hype-oriented methods doesn't produce the same depth of gospel transformation and then gospel transmission and multiplication as intentional and deeply relational life-on-life disciple making.

Hard work. Verse 6: "It is the hard-working farmer who ought to have the first share of the crops." We might want to call this "jolly hard work," because now in verse 6 Paul is drawing out the great joy at the end of disciple making, which is not material rewards but people rewards, strange as it may sound. It's being able to say, as Paul does in Philippians 4:1, that those in whom he has invested have become "my brothers, whom I love and long for, my joy and crown . . . my beloved." (Note the connection with the athlete's crown in verse 5.) It's the kind of reward that causes our mouths to fall open when we read in 1 Thessalonians 2:19–20, "What is our hope or joy or crown of boasting before our Lord Jesus at his coming? Is it not you? For you are our glory and joy."

The point Paul is getting at in these three illustrations is that entrusting the gospel in a few others who will invest in others also (v. 2) will mean sharing in Paul's own suffering (v. 3). There will be temptations to diversion, cutting corners, and laxity. But the mission of disciple making will take single-mindedness (v. 4), discipline (v. 5), and jolly hard work (v. 6), which leads us to this enigmatic verse 7.

Verse 7: "Think over what I say, for the Lord will give you understanding in everything." Here's how I think Paul might explain this verse in the context of what he's just said in verses 2–6. "Okay, Timothy, think over what I'm saying here. Jesus entrusted the gospel to me. I've given my life to entrusting it to others, to multiplying his message in others' lives, and what I've received for it in this life is suffering and prison." (Side note here: people don't often get too upset when you're just being a disciple, but when you start seriously giving yourself to making disciples—and disciples who make other disciples—suffering in some form is not too far around the corner. Back to Paul . . .) "And now, Timothy, I'm calling you not only to be a disciple—not only to guard the gospel and live it out—but to entrust it to others. To build it into others. To make disciples, to use Jesus's words. To work for gospel advance in a few specific lives, such that they in turn disciple others. And, Timothy, the path ahead will not be easy. It will require single-mindedness and discipline and hard work. As I have suffered, so you will suffer. Think over what I say, Timothy. I'm in prison for gospel advance and now I'm calling you to the same. Entrust the gospel to faithful men who will be able to teach others also and be ready for the suffering that will come with it in due course."[6]

So here's our call to suffering. Here's our call to do the hard thing: invest the gospel deeply in the lives of a few, such that they also will invest in a few, who invest in a few.[7]

So now we face this tension. We've seen that (1) we Christians are called to make disciples who make disciples, and that (2) disciple making is hard work and brings suffering. So now the issue is: Where do we get the resources for the tough task? Where do we find the strength to press through the resistance and hard work and pain and suffering and difficulty with single-mindedness and discipline in making disciples who make disciples? This brings us back to verse 1 and the final point of this appendix.

---

[6] Don't think of Christian suffering merely as something that happens when you do street preaching in a foreign country hostile to the gospel or when you're put down by others because you believe the gospel. Paul's suffering in 2 Timothy (being imprisoned) comes from doing what he charges Timothy to do in 2:2, namely, investing the gospel in those who will invest the gospel in others also. It's just everyday disciple making, making disciples who make disciples, that brings suffering—for Paul the suffering of prison and most often just the everyday difficulties and labor of verses 3–6. To use the language of the Great Commission, merely observing Jesus's commands is tough and might get you in trouble, but *teaching others* to observe all that he commanded—that will bring hardship, pain, suffering, toil, and perhaps prison in some societies.

[7] David Platt writes, "Making disciples is not an easy process. It is trying. It is messy. It is slow, tedious, even painful at times [might he have 2 Tim. 2:3–6 in mind here?]. It is all these things because it is relational. Jesus has not given us an effortless step-by-step formula for impacting nations for his glory. He has given us people, and he has said, 'Live for them. Love them, serve them, and lead them. Lead them to follow me, and lead them to lead others to follow me. In the process you will multiply the gospel to the ends of the earth.'" *Radical*, 93.

3) THE KEY TO DISCIPLE MAKING IS
GOSPEL GRACE (V. 1)

Verse 1: "You then, my child, be strengthened by *the grace that is in Christ Jesus.*" Disciple making is essential, and it's hard, but in Jesus is the grace for it—grace in several senses. As we saw earlier, the grace of the gospel is the content of disciple making, what we seek to pass along. The gospel is the deposit we entrust to others. We disciple grace—and not just general, ambiguous grace. Not laxity. But *the grace*, gospel grace.

And the grace of the gospel is not only the content of disciple making but also the power, the strength, and the energy for disciple making. "Be strengthened by the grace that is in Christ Jesus." Gospel grace is the fuel that runs the discipler's engine up the hills of resistance and hardship and pain and suffering and obscurity. This in particular is what Paul is getting at in verse 1 (as well as in 1:8, "share in suffering for the gospel by the power of God").

And notice that Paul doesn't say in verse 1, "Make yourself strong in Jesus's grace." Rather, it's *"be strengthened* by the grace"—not first a charge to act, but to be acted upon. Just as Jesus is the ultimate guarder of the gospel, as Paul mentions in 1:12, so also he's the ultimate advancer of the gospel, the one who promises, "I will build my church, and the gates of hell shall not prevail against it" (Matt. 16:18). Jesus is the one who empowers the mission through his blood-bought grace. Jesus does the strengthening for disciple making and doesn't leave us to muster up our own strength for the gospel's grunt work. He calls us to be receivers of his strength, not originators of our own. But how does this empowering happen? And here's where we end with the deepest sense of how gospel grace is the key to disciple making.

At the heart of how Jesus energizes us for the hard work of disciple making is our continual receiving of the grace of the gospel that covers our endless mistakes and failures in disciple making. And here's ultimately how the gospel and the cross and grace are central in disciple making—not merely in being the content, and not in being some kind of mystical empowerment, but in being the objective achievement of Jesus for us at the cross in history that covers our sins, and in doing so empowers us for the hard work of extending grace to others.

Begin the process of trying to build the full-orbed gospel relationally and intentionally into a younger believer and see how quickly and significantly you fail. If you want to destroy your perfectionism, take up disciple making. One of the few guarantees in disciple making is that we will not do it perfectly but poorly—and often, if not frequently, we will fail miserably. There has been only one perfect discipler, the One who gave his life to discipling only twelve men on his way to giving his life to accomplish our redemption. Paul says in 1:9–10, God "saved us . . . not because of our works"—not because of our disciple making!—"but because of his own purpose and grace, which he gave us in Christ Jesus before the ages began, and which now has been manifested through the appearing of our Savior Christ Jesus, who abolished death and brought life and immortality to light through the gospel." The ultimate disciple making of Jesus's life on earth ended with the ultimate disciple covering when he took our sins at the cross, including all our failures in discipling.

So Jesus is more than the perfect model of disciple making. He died to save sinners like us who even with new hearts prove so woefully inadequate in making disciples who make disciples. In the end, by his grace, gospel advance and disciple making are not on our shoulders. Jesus will build his church (Matt. 16:18). Jesus is the one who will guard the gospel he has entrusted to us (2 Tim. 1:12). Jesus is the ultimate empowerer of disciple making. And Jesus is the one whose cross covers all our many failures in, and through that cross energizes us for, making disciples who make other disciples of his lavish grace.

ACKNOWLEDGMENTS

We thank God for Crossway and for our ongoing partnership for the gospel. For Lane, Justin, Lydia, and the rest of the team for locking arms with us once again.

We thank God for Bethlehem, our church here in the Twin Cities—John's home for over three decades, David's for almost a decade. For a generally happy people, for forty fellow elders, and for the weekly corporate-worship manifestations of the vision in Minneapolis, Mounds View, and Lakeville.

We thank God for Desiring God, which hosts the National Conference each fall from which these revised and expanded messages originally came. For Jon Bloom, Scott Anderson, Josh Etter, and conference director Dave Clifford. And for Bill Walsh, who pioneered "International Outreach" at Desiring God, an initiative that now shapes everything we do at DG and has given birth to a larger international focus and ministry with The Gospel Coalition. Bill was instrumental in turning our attention to this theme for the 2011 National Conference and for coalescing the partnerships that made the event so significant.

We thank God for our wives and our families, who daily strengthen and sustain us, and gently, but firmly, remind us not to outrun the supply lines as we press ever forward in the mission.

Finally, and most significantly, we thank God for him who has given us strength, Christ Jesus our Lord. Only through him can we do all things—be brought low, abound, face plenty and hunger, abundance and need. Only through him do we have confidence that the unengaged and unreached will be engaged and reached.

He is the one who has promised to build his church. He is the one who ensures the gospel will be preached throughout the whole world, as a testimony to all the nations, and then the end will come. He is the one who never lies and most certainly, as surely as he is God, will finish the mission.

David Mathis and John Piper
Minneapolis, Minnesota
May 25, 2012

SUBJECT INDEX

NAME INDEX

SCRIPTURE INDEX

❄ desiringGod

If you would like to explore further the vision of God and life presented in this book, we at Desiring God would love to serve you. We have thousands of resources to help you grow in your passion for Jesus Christ and help you spread that passion to others. At our website, www.desiringGod.org, you'll find almost everything John Piper has written and preached, including more than forty books. We've made over thirty years of his sermons available free online for you to read, listen to, download, and in some cases watch.

In addition, you can access hundreds of articles, find out where John Piper is speaking, learn about our conferences, and browse our online store. John Piper receives no royalties from the books he writes and no compensation from Desiring God. The funds are all reinvested into our gospel-spreading efforts. Desiring God also has a whatever-you-can-afford policy, designed for individuals with limited discretionary funds. If you'd like more information about this policy, please contact us at the address or phone number below. We exist to help you treasure Jesus Christ and his gospel above all things because he is most glorified in you when you are most satisfied in him. Let us know how we can serve you!

Desiring God
Post Office Box 2901 Minneapolis, Minnesota 55402
888.346.4700   mail@desiringGod.org